Exercise for Mood and Anxiety Disorde

Exercise for Mood and Anxiety Disorders

Therapist Guide

Jasper A. J. Smits • Michael W. Otto

OXFORD

UNIVERSITY PRESS

2009

OXFORD

UNIVERSITY PRESS

Oxford University Press, Inc., publishes works that further
Oxford University's objective of excellence
in research, scholarship, and education.

Oxford   New York
Auckland   Cape Town   Dar es Salaam   Hong Kong   Karachi
Kuala Lumpur   Madrid   Melbourne   Mexico City   Nairobi
New Delhi   Shanghai   Taipei   Toronto

With offices in
Argentina   Austria   Brazil   Chile   Czech Republic   France   Greece
Guatemala   Hungary   Italy   Japan   Poland   Portugal   Singapore
South Korea   Switzerland   Thailand   Turkey   Ukraine   Vietnam

Copyright © 2009 by Oxford University Press, Inc.

Published by Oxford University Press, Inc.
198 Madison Avenue, New York, New York 10016

www.oup.com

Oxford is a registered trademark of Oxford University Press

Library of Congress Cataloging-in-Publication Data
Smits, Jasper A. J.
Exercise for mood and anxiety disorders : therapist guide / Jasper A. J. Smits, Michael W. Otto.
p.   cm. — (TreatmentsThatWork)
Includes bibliographical references and index.
ISBN 978-0-19-538225-9
1. Mood (Psychology)   2. Exercise therapy.   3. Exercise—Psychological aspects.
I. Otto, Michael W.   II. Title.
BF521.S65 2009
616.89′0642—dc22

2009000271

9   8   7   6   5   4   3   2   1

Printed in the United States of America
on acid-free paper

About Treatments *ThatWork*™

Stunning developments in healthcare have taken place over the last several years, but many of our widely accepted interventions and strategies in mental health and behavioral medicine have been brought into question by research evidence as not only lacking benefit, but perhaps, inducing harm. Other strategies have been proven effective using the best current standards of evidence, resulting in broad-based recommendations to make these practices more available to the public. Several recent developments are behind this revolution. First, we have arrived at a much deeper understanding of pathology, both psychological and physical, which has led to the development of new, more precisely targeted interventions. Second, our research methodologies have improved substantially, such that we have reduced threats to internal and external validity, making the outcomes more directly applicable to clinical situations. Third, governments around the world and healthcare systems and policymakers have decided that the quality of care should improve, that it should be evidence based, and that it is in the public's interest to ensure that this happens (Barlow, 2004; Institute of Medicine, 2001).

Of course, the major stumbling block for clinicians everywhere is the accessibility of newly developed evidence-based psychological interventions. Workshops and books can go only so far in acquainting responsible and conscientious practitioners with the latest behavioral healthcare practices and their applicability to individual patients. This new series, Treatments *ThatWork*™, is devoted to communicating these exciting new interventions to clinicians on the frontlines of practice.

The manuals and workbooks in this series contain step-by-step detailed procedures for assessing and treating specific problems and diagnoses. But this series also goes beyond the books and manuals by providing ancillary materials that will approximate the supervisory process in assisting practitioners in the implementation of these procedures in their practice.

In our emerging healthcare system, the growing consensus is that evidence-based practice offers the most responsible course of action for the mental health professional. All behavioral healthcare clinicians deeply desire to provide the best possible care for their patients. In this series, our aim is to close the dissemination and information gap and make that possible.

One of the best kept secrets in the treatment of mood and anxiety disorders is the proven efficacy of a program of exercise, which has many benefits on mood, but has yet to be widely adopted as a therapeutic technique. This therapist guide provides guidance for care providers who want to apply exercise-based interventions to the treatment of mood and anxiety disorders.

The interventions described can be applied in a variety of settings ranging from primary care to specialty care in the context of psychological, psychiatric, nursing, or social work settings. Treatment is organized around a weekly prescribed activity program, with an emphasis on teaching clients strategies for staying motivated and organized in order to ensure adherence to the program. The introductory chapters describe the intervention and how to initiate it with clients, while later chapters focus specifically on using exercise to combat depression, as well as stress, worry, and panic. This guide provides an integrated approach to establish exercise programs targeting mood and anxiety disorders, and also provides useful cognitive and behavioral interventions designed to support these programs.

David H. Barlow, Editor-in-Chief,
Treatments *ThatWork*™
Boston, MA

References

Barlow, D. H. (2004). Psychological treatments. *American Psychologist, 59,* 869–878.

Institute of Medicine. (2001). *Crossing the quality chasm: A new health system for the 21st century.* Washington, DC: National Academy Press.

Dedications

JAJS: To Jill and Stella, for many happy exercise sessions

MWO: To Jenni, for the laughter and joy she brings

Acknowledgments

Our writing of the therapist guide and workbook for *Exercise for Mood and Anxiety Disorders* was motivated by research showing the tremendous benefits of exercise for mental health and well-being. We want to acknowledge the valuable evidence provided by international teams of researchers who documented these benefits in population-based studies, experimental investigations, clinical studies, meta-analytical comparisons, and review articles. We would also like to thank our collaborators on our own investigations in this area. In particular, our collaborators on research and review articles included Evi Behar, Angie Berry, Tim Church, Lynette Craft, Daniel Galper, Dina Gordon, Tracy Greer, Pamela Handelsman, Bridget Hearon, Kristin Julian, Kate McHugh, Alicia Meuret, Heather Murray, Mark Powers, Katherine Presnell, David Rosenfield, Anke Seidel, Georgia Stathopoulou, Candyce Tart, Madhukar Trivedi, and Michael Zvolensky. All of these individuals helped expand what is known about the benefits of exercise for mood and anxiety disorders.

Contents

Chapter 1   *Introductory Information for Therapists*

Background Information and Purpose of This Program

This therapist guide and the accompanying patient workbook provide guidance for care providers and patients who want to apply exercise-based interventions to the treatment of mood and anxiety disorders. Despite the striking evidence for efficacy (Stathopoulou, Powers, Berry, Smits, & Otto, 2006), it is clear that exercise interventions for affective disorders have not been widely adopted for use by primary care clinicians or mental health specialists. Given the obvious benefits of exercise for stress, mood, and anxiety management, combined with the benefits for physical health and well-being, there is a clear need for adoption of exercise-based interventions across the range of settings where patients seek help. This manual aids this adoption, providing guidance in integrating exercise-based interventions with mental health care.

This guide to exercise interventions for mood and anxiety disorders is designed for a wide range of care providers. First, it is designed for application in a variety of settings ranging from primary care to specialty care in the context of psychological, psychiatric, nursing, or social work settings. Second, exercise interventions are compatible with diverse care philosophies. For example, those who organize their care around the latest in empirical findings can provide exercise interventions that are known for reliably strong effect sizes for the benefit provided to patients with mood disorders (see section "Efficacy of Exercise Interventions"). Likewise, for providers who attend to a mind–body connection and are seeking a holistic treatment approach to patient care, exercise interventions provide a means by which to engage the patient's body in treatment while ensuring a focus on affect and cognition. For those who provide psychotherapy, exercise provides a balanced intervention focused on acting and experiencing rather than on thinking and feeling. For those who provide pharmacotherapy, exercise helps ensure an active engagement of the patient in mental and physical health promotion that has efficacy in the same range as that of antidepressant treatments (Stathopoulou et al., 2006).

Treatment is organized around providing the evidence-based dose of exercise per week, while helping patients with the variety of motivational and organizational issues that can derail exercise interventions before they are established as a healthful habit. Recognizing that the adoption of an exercise habit is difficult, especially for persons with anxiety and mood disorders (Goodwin, 2003; Schmitz, Kruse, & Kugler, 2004), specific strategies for helping the patient process her exercise experiences to enhance motivation for subsequent activity are provided. The cognitive and problem-solving interventions that support the core exercise program are exemplified in this guide and are further supported with detailed information, examples, and worksheets in the corresponding patient workbook. As such, this manual provides an integrated approach to establish exercise programs targeting mood and anxiety disorders and also provides useful cognitive and behavioral interventions designed to support these programs.

Nature and Significance of Mood and Anxiety Disorders

Mood disorders include unipolar depressive and bipolar disorders. The distinction between the two is that bipolar disorder involves manic or hypomanic episodes, whereas unipolar depression involves depression only. Unipolar depression is more common relative to bipolar disorder, with lifetime prevalence rates of 16.8%, 2.8%, and 4.4% for major depressive disorder, dysthymia, and any bipolar disorder (e.g., bipolar I, bipolar II, or subthreshold bipolar disorder), respectively (Kessler, Berglund, et al., 2005; Merikangas et al., 2007). Approximately half of the individuals who have had a first episode of depression recover, while the other half either does not remit or has recurrent episodes (Eaton et al., 2008). Bipolar disorders tend to be chronic and recurrent (Judd et al., 2002; 2003), and all mood disorders are associated with significant comorbidity (Kessler, Chiu, Demler, Merikangas, & Walters, 2005) and high societal costs (Simon, 2003; Stewart, Ricci, Chee, Hahn, & Morganstein, 2003).

Anxiety disorders represent a broad class of *DSM-IV Axis-I disorders*, including panic disorder (with or without agoraphobia), agoraphobia without a history of panic disorder, specific phobia, social phobia, obsessive-compulsive disorder (OCD), post-traumatic stress disorder, acute stress disorder, and generalized anxiety disorder. These anxiety disorders share in common sympathetic activation, worry or hypervigilance, and avoidance and differ primarily in the content or focus of the apprehension (e.g., fear of panic in panic disorder vs. fear of negative evaluation in social phobia). The prevalence rate of an anxiety disorder in one's lifetime is 28.8% (Kessler et al., 2005). Lifetime prevalence rates across the anxiety disorders range from 1.4% for agoraphobia without panic disorder to 12.5% for specific phobia. Anxiety disorders frequently co-occur with other psychiatric and medical conditions, tend to be chronic when left untreated (Bruce et al., 2005; Kessler et al., 2005; Roy-Byrne et al., 2008), and are associated with significant societal costs (Greenberg et al., 1999).

Problem Focus

Despite having established efficacy, contemporary single or combined pharmacological and psychosocial interventions for mood and anxiety disorders leave ample room for improvement. Indeed, large clinical trials indicate that a significant number of patients either fail to respond or remain symptomatic after treatment completion (deRubeis, Gelfand, Tang, & Simons, 1999; Hofmann & Smits, 2008; Lydiard et al., 1996; Otto, Smits & Reese, 2005; Thase & Denko, 2008). Accordingly, for many patients, achieving remission requires the use of strategies that can augment established interventions. As we describe in greater detail later on, exercise interventions have emerged as a viable alternative or complementary strategy.

The use of exercise in the treatment of mood and anxiety disorders (either as a single modality or in combination with established interventions) may also enhance the appeal of treatment to many patients and treatment providers, thereby increasing access to and utilization of effective care. There has been a tremendous rise in demand among the general public for contemporary and alternative treatments such as exercise-based interventions (Eisenberg et al., 1998). More than half of individuals who suffer from depression or anxiety report using alternative treatments for relief of their symptoms (Kessler et al., 2001). In addition to the reduced social stigma associated with exercise interventions, many patients are likely drawn to this approach because it requires their active participation in the healing process and fits with their often-held assumption that overcoming (mental) health problems requires treatment of the whole person, which may be better achieved using natural remedies (Bishop, Yardley, & Lewith, 2007). This holistic approach inherent to exercise interventions is also appealing to providers as they aim to help patients with anxiety and depression improve their overall quality of life, especially considering that exercise interventions have established clear efficacy for improving physical health and general well-being (Dishman, Heath, & Washburn, 2004).

Mechanism of Exercise Effects on Mood and Anxiety

The use of exercise interventions for mood and anxiety disorders is supported by advances in the understanding of biological and psychological processes underlying the improvement in these conditions. Specifically, several sources of evidence point to the ability of exercise to target core processes believed to be important for therapeutic change for mood and anxiety disorders. For example, animal studies and some preliminary work with humans suggest that exercise results in changes in activity in both noradrenergic and serotonergic systems (Chaouloff, 1997; Dey, Singh, & Dey, 1992; Dishman, 1997; Dunn, Reigle, Youngstedt, Armstrong, & Dishman, 1996; Pagliari & Peyrin, 1995), both of which have been implicated in mood and anxiety disorders. Accordingly, exercise may be conceptualized as a non-pharmacological equivalent of antidepressant medication, which is presumed to exert its effects by modifying these systems.

Another physiological change mechanism, which has also been suggested to underlie the effects of certain antidepressants (Vogel, 1983), may be the normalization of the disrupted sleep cycle, which is commonly observed among persons with depression and anxiety (Casper et al., 1994; Driver & Taylor, 2000; Kubitz, Landers, Petruzzello, & Han, 1996; Tanaka & Shirakawa, 2004). This proposed mechanism is in line with the social zeitgeber theory (Ehlers, Frank, & Kupfer, 1988; Ehlers, Kupfer, Frank, & Monk, 1993), which posits that activities such as exercise may improve the regularity of daily lifestyles, which in turn improves and helps stabilize mood. Initial support for this mediational hypothesis comes from a randomized controlled investigation involving depressed adults, which indicated that exercise was associated with significant improvements in subjective sleep quality and corresponding improvements in self-reported symptoms of depression (Singh, Clements, & Fiatarone, 1997).

Exercise interventions can be used as a means to provide patients with the learning experiences that appear central to the efficacy of psychotherapeutic approaches to mood and anxiety disorders. Indeed, the act of engaging in exercise facilitates the goal to replace the maladaptive action tendencies of depression (i.e., passivity) with functional actions (i.e., activation), thereby helping the patient reestablish adaptive positive activities. From this perspective—that is, enhancing persistence in the face of discomfort—exercise interventions are similar to established behavioral activation treatments for depression (for review, see Hopko, Lejeuz, Ruggiero, & Eifert, 2003; Jacobson, Martell, & Dimidjian, 2001). In a similar fashion, highly moderate- to vigorous-intensity exercise can be used as an interoceptive exposure strategy (i.e., approach) for patients with anxiety disorders who fear (and avoid) anxiety and related bodily sensations. In other words, by engaging in this type of exercise, patients will receive exposure to a number of anxiety-related sensations (e.g., racing heart, rapid breathing, and sweating), which allows the fears of these sensations to dissipate. Support for the use of exercise to provide interoceptive exposure comes from a series of recently completed randomized controlled studies. Specifically, three studies have demonstrated that a brief exercise program (i.e., six 20-min sessions of moderate- to vigorous-intensity treadmill exercise [60–80% of age-adjusted maximum heart rate]) outperforms waitlist (Broman-Fulks & Storey, 2008; Smits et al., 2008) and low dose exercise (i.e., six 20-min sessions of light-intensity treadmill exercise [<60% of age-adjusted maximum heart rate]; Broman-Fulks, Berman, Rabian, & Webster (2004)) in reducing the fear of anxiety and related bodily sensations (i.e., anxiety sensitivity) among healthy adults with clinical levels of anxiety sensitivity. Evidence further suggests that the improvements in anxiety sensitivity observed with exercise guide subsequent changes in depressed mood and anxiety (Smits et al., 2008). These findings bear relevance to the treatment of not only panic disorder, but also other anxiety disorders (e.g., social phobia, post-traumatic stress disorder, and generalized anxiety disorder), major depressive disorder, and bipolar illness, all of which are characterized by elevations in anxiety sensitivity (Cox, Enns, Freeman, & Walker, 2001; Otto, Pollack, Fava, & Uccello, 1995; Simon et al., 2005; Taylor, Koch, & McNally, 1992).

Efficacy of Exercise Interventions

Evidence from a variety of sources has consistently pointed to the anxiolytic and antidepressant properties of exercise. Several large cross-sectional population studies have demonstrated that individuals who exercise report fewer symptoms of anxiety and depression (Stephens, 1988) and lower levels of stress, anger, and cynical distrust (Hassmen, Koivula, & Uutela, 2000) relative to their counterparts who do not exercise. Using data from the National Comorbidity Survey, Goodwin (2003) found that regular physical activity predicted lower prevalence of current major depression (OR = 0.75), panic attacks (OR = 0.73), social phobia (OR = 0.65), specific phobia (OR = 0.78), and agoraphobia (OR = 0.64), even after controlling for demographic variables and comorbid physical and mental health conditions. Interestingly, there was also evidence for a dose–response relationship between physical activity and mental health problems in this study, such that the lowest prevalence rates of anxiety and mood disorders were observed among persons who exercised regularly, followed by those who exercised occasionally, rarely, and never, respectively. Prospective large-scale studies have further shown that physical activity is associated with a reduced risk of developing depression (Camacho, Roberts, Lazarus,

Kaplan, & Cohen, 1991; Paffenbarger, Lee, & Leung, 1994), after controlling for demographic variables (Farmer, Locke, Moscicki, Larson, & Radloff, 1998).

There are numerous studies that have experimentally manipulated physical activity, providing some evidence for the causal effects of physical activity on depressed mood and anxiety. In a meta-analytic study of studies examining the effects of exercise for reducing anxiety, Petruzzello, Landers, Hatfield, Kubitz, and Salazar (1991) found that randomized controlled investigations yielded an average effect size in the medium range of $d = 0.54$ for the advantage of exercise over control conditions. Similarly, Craft and Landers (1998) reported a large effect size ($d = 0.77$) for exercise interventions relative to waitlist control conditions and comparable efficacy to treatment comparison conditions ($d = 0.05$) for reducing symptoms of depression. It should be noted that most of the studies included in these meta-analyses involved nonclinical samples, although there is some evidence, at least for treating anxiety, that the benefits of exercise are greater among highly anxious samples. One implication of this finding is that the degree of benefit from exercise may be much more profound in clinical populations.

The results from these correlational large-scale studies and experimental studies involving mostly nonclinical samples are nicely complemented by a series of randomized controlled trials with diagnosed patients and have helped confirm that programmed aerobic exercise has consistent effects on promoting well-being in patients with mood and anxiety disorders.

Major Depressive Disorder

A number of randomized controlled investigations of exercise interventions for major depression have been completed in the past two decades. Recently, we meta-analytically reviewed the findings of trials ($n = 11$) that compared exercise programs to nonactive comparison conditions (e.g., waitlist or placebo treatment, low-level exercise, and health education; Stathopoulou et al., 2006). The exercise interventions employed in the sample studies varied with respect to the frequency of exercise

Model	Study	Hedges' g and 95% CI

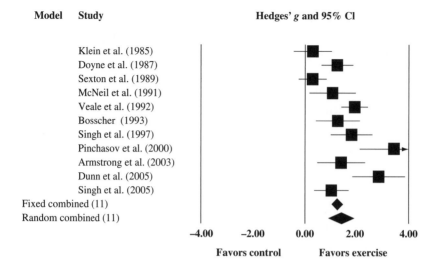

Figure 1.1

Effect Sizes for the Benefits of Exercise for Major Depression

(twice to four times a week) as well as the duration (20–45 min) and the intensity (up to 70–85% of the maximum heart rate) of the exercise session. Attrition analyses revealed that the average dropout rate for the exercise interventions is comparable to that observed for psychotherapy and pharmacological interventions. Specifically, on average, 19.9% of patients receiving exercise did not complete the intervention. This rate was identical to the control condition. Figure 1.1 displays a forest plot of controlled effect sizes of improvements in depressed mood, with 95% confidence interval for each study. Random effects analysis revealed a large mean overall between-group effect size ($g = 1.39$ or $d = 1.42$), indicating a significant advantage of exercise interventions over control conditions. Not surprisingly, the effect sizes tended to be larger when compared to wait-list or no-treatment conditions (mean $g = 1.64$, $n = 5$) as compared to the other control conditions (mean $g = 1.17$, $n = 6$).

The question as to whether the effects of aerobic exercise on depression are dose dependent has been addressed in only one study to date. In a randomized placebo-controlled study involving 80 patients with mild to moderate severity of major depression (i.e., HRSD17 > 16), Dunn, Trivedi, Kampert, Clark, and Chambliss (2005) found that the public health-recommended dose of aerobic exercise (total energy expenditure of 17.5 kcal/kg/week) yielded greater reductions (47%) in depression compared to low-dose exercise (total energy expenditure 7.0 kcal/kg/week; 30%), which did not outperform the activity-based placebo (29%). Much like the study of the dose–response relationship, the studies investigating the relative efficacy of different exercise modalities (e.g., aerobic vs. anaerobic) are limited in number. Results of two small-scale randomized controlled studies (Doyne et al., 1987; Martinsen, Hoffart, & Solberg, 1989) suggested that aerobic exercise does not outperform anaerobic exercise in reducing depressed mood, although Martinsen and colleagues (1989) found, consistent with extant data, that aerobic exercise was associated with greater improvements in physical fitness (Martinsen et al., 1989).

Bipolar Depression

The success of exercise interventions for the treatment of major depressive disorder has stimulated research of the use of exercise for the treatment of bipolar illness. Recently, Ng, Dodd, and Berk (2007) reported the results of a pilot investigation involving 98 patients with bipolar depression admitted to inpatient care. Employing a retrospective research design, they compared the clinical status at discharge of patients who regularly participated in an exercise program to that of patients who did not participate. The exercise program consisted of a nurse-led walking group that met every weekday morning for 40 min. The intensity of walking depended on the physical abilities of the participants. Although the groups did not show differential improvement on measures of global improvement (e.g., CGI-I, CGI-S), participants participating in the exercise program reported significantly greater improvements in depression, anxiety, and stress.

Exercise interventions for bipolar disorder are also encouraged by the finding that treatments for unipolar depression have extensions to bipolar depression (Zaretsky, Segal, & Gemar, 1999) and that interventions that help balance activities and the sleep–wake cycle may be especially important for patients with bipolar disorder (Frank et al., 1997). As such, the efficacy of exercise for patients with unipolar depression may extend to those with bipolar depression (for review, see Otto & Miklowitz, 2004), and exercise may offer additional mood-stabilizing properties due to its effects on stress, sleep, and social rhythms.

Anxiety Disorders

The investigation of the efficacy of exercise interventions for treating anxiety has mostly involved samples of patients suffering from panic disorder, although there is some data available pertinent to other anxiety disorders, including social phobia, generalized anxiety disorder, and OCD. The first randomized controlled study compared the efficacy of an aerobic exercise intervention to that of a non-aerobic exercise program among patients with panic disorder along with agoraphobia ($n = 56$), social phobia, ($n = 13$) or generalized anxiety disorder ($n = 10$). Both interventions involved weekly 1-hr group sessions (of which 30 min were devoted to exercise) for an eight-week period. The intensity of aerobic exercise was set at 70% of maximal aerobic capacity (e.g., brisk walking, running), whereas the intensity of the anaerobic program, which comprised muscular strength training, was unspecified. The posttreatment results indicated no differences between the two groups in improvements on anxiety measures, although aerobic exercise was associated with greater improvements in cardiorespiratory fitness. Importantly, the overall attrition rate was relatively low (11%). Interestingly, dropout in this study was evident only among patients with panic disorder ($n = 9$; 16%), perhaps suggesting that initiating exercise interventions with patients with panic disorder may offer some challenges relative to working with other anxiety patients.

As outlined in greater detail in Chapter 5, it may be important to provide patients with panic disorder a model for the use of exercise for reducing their panic and related anxiety. Indeed, patients with panic disorder have been shown to avoid exercise because they are often concerned about the consequences of bodily sensations (e.g., racing heart, rapid breathing) (Smits & Zvolensky, 2006; Schmidt et al., 2000). Accordingly, patients may be more likely to adhere to the intervention if provided with the rationale that exposure to bodily sensations through exercise will result in anxiety but ultimately help them learn that these sensations are not dangerous.

Evidence consistent with the idea that patients with panic disorder may do better with exercise interventions if provided a model comes from a study by Broocks and colleagues (1998). In a 10-week randomized placebo-controlled trial involving 46 patients with panic disorder, they compared the efficacy of aerobic exercise to that of clomipramine or pill placebo. Aerobic exercise intervention consisted of a combined supervised and home-based walking or running program. Patients completed a self-selected four-mile route (forest or park) that was easily accessible from their home at least three times a week, where walking was allowed during the first 6 weeks and running was expected during the last 4 weeks. In addition, they met with a trainer once each week to run together. At posttreatment, both active treatments outperformed the placebo condition and were equally effective in reducing anxiety, although clomipramine yielded greater changes in global improvement ratings relative to the exercise intervention. The dropout rate was 31% for the exercise group, 0% for the clomipramine group, and 27% for the placebo group. The authors further noted that avoidance of more intense exercise was evident in a subset of the patients and suggested that additional cognitive interventions (i.e., preparing them to reappraise some of the feared consequences of exercise-induced sensations) would possibly have enhanced the benefits among participants in the exercise condition.

Initial feasibility data also supports the use of exercise in the treatment of OCD. In an open trial involving 15 patients who were on a stable dose of cognitive-behavioral therapy, pharmacotherapy, or their combination, Brown and colleagues (2007) examined the effects of a 12-week combined supervised and home-based aerobic exercise intervention. Patients progressed from 20-min to 40-min exercise sessions (at 55–69% of age-predicted maximal heart rate) three to four times a week. Supervised group sessions also included a 30-min meeting with a clinical psychologist and an exercise physiologist to discuss topics related to compliance with the intervention program (e.g., benefits of exercise, goal setting, and identifying and overcoming barriers to exercise). Acute and follow-up effect sizes for reductions in Y-BOCS scores were in the large range (e.g., $d = 1.69$ from pre- to posttreatment; and $d = 1.11$ for pretreatment to 6-month follow-up). Moreover, clinically meaningful changes were observed for 69% and 50% of patients at posttreatment and 6-month follow-up, respectively.

Risks and Benefits of This Treatment Program

The risk associated with exercise varies as a function of the combination of exercise intensity and the individual's age and health status. The American Heart Association (AHA) and the American College of Sports Medicine (ACSM) recommend that the start of an exercise program be preceded by an assessment of risk, which can be performed using a questionnaire such as the Physical Activity Readiness Questionnaire (PAR-Q).

Physical Activity Readiness Questionnaire (PAR-Q)

If you are between the ages of 15 and 69, the PAR-Q will tell you if you should check with your doctor before engaging in physical activity. Common sense is your best guide when you answer these questions. Please read them carefully and answer each one honestly by checking Yes or No.

Yes   No

☐   ☐   1. Has your doctor ever said that you have a heart condition and that you should only do physical activity recommended by a doctor?

☐   ☐   2. Do you feel pain in your chest when you do physical activity?

☐   ☐   3. In the past month, have you had chest pain when you were not doing physical activity?

☐   ☐   4. Do you lose your balance because of dizziness or do you ever lose consciousness?

☐   ☐   5. Do you have a bone or joint problem (e.g., back, knee, or hip) that could be made worse by a change in your physical activity?

☐   ☐   6. Is your doctor currently prescribing drugs (e.g., water pills) for high blood pressure or heart condition?

☐   ☐   7. Do you know of any other reason why you should not engage in physical activity?

If you answered Yes to one or more questions, talk to your doctor **before** beginning a physical activity program.

If you answered No to all questions, you can be reasonably sure that you can start becoming more physically active.

Generally, asymptomatic men <45 years of age and asymptomatic women <55 years of age with no risk factors do not need to consult with a physician before beginning a moderate-intensity exercise program. Those who do endorse symptoms and risk factors or have any chronic disease or medical problems should obtain medical clearance. This step is also recommended for men > 45 years of age and women >55 years of age as well as for sedentary persons who plan to initiate a program that includes vigorous-intensity exercise.

The benefits of programmed exercise include not only improvements in mood and anxiety, but also improvements in physical health and general well-being. As such, this intervention offers the opportunity to address multiple mental and physical health conditions simultaneously. To providers, this program may be particularly appealing because it is easy to implement in a variety of settings and it is easy to learn. For patients, exercise interventions may be appealing because of the reduced stigma associated with such interventions relative to other established treatments for mood and anxiety disorders.

Alternative Treatments

As discussed previously, there is a wealth of evidence supporting cognitive-behavioral as well as pharmacologic interventions for mood and anxiety disorders. Also, interpersonal psychotherapy (IPT) has demonstrated efficacy for the treatment of depression. Exercise interventions offer a treatment strategy that is alternative or adjunctive to these approaches. As an alternative strategy, exercise may be an acceptable treatment modality among patients who are unwilling to commit to pharmacotherapy or psychotherapy, and, due to the limited number of sessions needed, it may be a cost-effective alternative. As an adjunctive treatment, exercise may be considered when response to more traditional treatments is lagging or when therapists wish to provide a broader or more holistic approach in addition to their core modality of treatment. In every case, exercise should be considered in relation to other available treatments and patient preference, with ongoing monitoring of outcomes and the need for alternative interventions.

Outline of This Treatment Program

Once it has been determined that exercise is a safe activity for the patient, the treatment program can be initiated. In the subsequent chapters, we describe the rationale for the exercise program, the appropriate planning for inevitable motivational issues (Chapter 2), the specifics of the exercise prescription (e.g., dose, initiation, and maintenance; Chapter 3), and the strategies specific to the treatment of mood and anxiety disorders (Chapters 4 and 5). The final chapter (Chapter 6) describes strategies designed to enhance adherence to the program and support the establishment of the new physical activity habit.

Use of the Patient Workbook

The patient workbook was developed to aid the adoption of exercise among patients participating in this program. The workbook provides patients with a wealth of information that complements the information provided by the therapist. The workbook also includes worksheets and logs to aid planning and monitoring of the patient's exercise program. Use of the workbook will help therapists deliver exercise prescriptions that are tailored to the needs of patients with mood and anxiety disorders.

Chapter 2   *Preparing for the Exercise Prescription*

(Corresponds to chapters 1–4 of the workbook)

Materials Needed

- Copy of patient workbook
- Valued Activities form
- Daily Schedule Planner

Outline

- Orient the patient to the program and identify mood symptoms for treatment
- Introduce a model for exercise interventions in response to negative mood states
- Present a model for motivation management
- Introduce the concept of a support team
- Review common barriers to exercise programs
- Introduce self-coaching strategies
- Introduce behavioral chaining strategies

Orienting the Patient to Exercise Treatment

Exercise-based treatment for mood and anxiety disorders is initiated by providing patients with accurate expectations about both the benefits and barriers to a successful exercise program. Discussions of benefits are directed to the efficacy of exercise for treating mood and anxiety disorders, as well as the general benefits to the management of subsyndromal symptoms and stress. Discussion of barriers includes emphasizing the role of motivation and the importance of *context* and *behavioral chaining* in making low-motivation activities easier to achieve. Moreover, in addition to the actual exercise prescription, treatment in this program is directed toward helping individuals get the most out of exercise by programming post-exercise cognitive processing and exercise-friendly activities.

The patient workbook is designed to support all of these interventions so that after receiving information directly from the therapist, patients are provided with complementary information as well as worksheets for monitoring and problem solving. Much of this information is to be provided before the initiation of exercise, so that exercise can be initiated with realistic expectations and a plan for success. Elements of this plan prominently include planning for a support network for exercise, planning a schedule for exercise, preparing for cognitive barriers for exercise, and developing a better self-coaching cognitive style for motivating, experiencing, and reviewing exercise experiences. These elements are discussed in the sections that follow.

The delivery of these preparatory interventions for exercise can be achieved across one or several sessions, depending on whether exercise is a primary or adjunctive intervention. However, the presumption is that in all cases, attention will be devoted to motivations and barriers for exercise interventions before the actual prescription of exercise.

Exercising for Mood: Short- Versus Long-Term Goals

A key goal of early informational discussions is to help patients achieve a fresh perspective on the nature of exercise for mental health. If physical health, rather than mood improvement, is the goal, individuals need to sustain an exercise program for an extended period of time before outcomes are achieved. That is, no matter the quality of any individual exercise session, changes in weight and physical health require extended effort over time. In contrast, when exercising for mood goals, individuals have the opportunity to examine how each individual session of exercise impacts their mood, anxiety, and stress levels. A great workout may leave individuals feeling transformed by that session and more willing to engage in the rest of a program of exercise treatment. In this sense, exercise is much more like programs of brief therapy where early changes in mood can redouble motivation and a sense of connection to the treatment and predict short- and long-term success in the treatment program (e.g., Tang & DeRubeis, 1999; Tang, DeRubeis, Hollon, Amsterdam, & Shelton, 2007). Also, according to clinical trial data, mood goals are achieved within the same time frame as that in acute treatment trials for medications or cognitive-behavioral therapy (CBT); e.g., beneficial results are evident well within 12 weeks of treatment of depression (Dunn et al., 2005) and 8 weeks of treatment of panic disorder (Broocks et al., 1998). Also, to the extent that negative mood states are part of the barriers to regular motivation for exercise, this program employs a type of *motivational judo*. Instead of perceiving a bad mood or poor motivation as a barrier to exercise, these mood and emotional states *are the very reason to exercise*. You may use the following sample dialogue to introduce this concept to the patient:

> *Exercise for a goal like weight loss or improved health is difficult because you need to complete many individual exercise sessions, over a course of weeks or months, to be able to achieve these gains. These benefits are very worthwhile, but when you know you have a long road of exercise ahead before you achieve benefits, it is very easy to put off any one single exercise session, saying "it won't matter" or "I don't feel like it now, maybe I will feel more like it next week." The sense that many people have is that with months of exercise in front of you, any missed session this week is not that important. This type of thinking can go a long way to derailing an individual's exercise program.*

> *But the good news is that the motivation to exercise can feel very different than that for physical health. When exercising for mood improvement, feeling bad, feeling tired, or feeling poorly motivated IS the very reason to exercise. And at each session of exercise, you have an opportunity to make yourself feel very different today, this very hour. Under these conditions, it is much harder to put off exercise, because it*

feels like you are putting off the chance of feeling better today. I want you to think of exercise as a way of transforming your mood state across the exercise session. This does not mean that exercise treats depression or anxiety in individual sessions, it is just that each session will leave you feeling different than when you started, and this change can help you chain together lots of exercise sessions for more long lasting and useful changes in mood.

This discussion—where motivation to exercise is linked explicitly to the negative mood states that typically derail exercise attempts—should be held in relation to the patient's stated goals of mood improvement. Some sections of Chapter 1 of the patient workbook are devoted to helping patients review their motivation for exercise and build a support team for their exercise program. The Symptoms to be Targeted by Exercise worksheet asks patients to self-identify the mood and anxiety symptoms they wish to target, and the information in that chapter continues the argument that whereas a regular program of exercise will bring longer-term health benefits, which include cardiovascular fitness, weight loss, greater strength and endurance, lower cholesterol and hypertension, enhanced immune function, and a prolonged life span, the goal of this exercise program is not simply targeted to these longer-term health benefits. For *this program*, the goal of exercise is to feel better *now*. Nonetheless, patients should be assured that when you exercise for mood, not only are you likely to feel better, you are likely to have better health and a longer life span during which you will be feeling better.

Considering Your Patient's Exercise Team

In preparation for exercise, therapists also need to help patients construct their support team and a broader set of goals that both support and reflect the mood changes their exercise habit can effect. The support team includes those individuals who will encourage the patient's program of exercise, support the program at times of lagging motivation, or participate directly in exercise activities with the patient. The Selecting Members of Your Support Team worksheet in Chapter 1 of the workbook provides the patient with a space to record the names of individuals selected for the support team. It is the therapist's role to discuss with the patient the realistic roles these individuals can take in providing support. The following questions can help elicit individuals who may be useful for the patient's team:

- *Who will be happy when your mood is improving?*

- *Who in your life is supportive of your goals?*

- *Who in your life is already exercising or who values the benefits of exercise?*

In discussing the patient's support team, keep in mind the findings on contagion of weight gain, where Christakis and Fowler (2007) found evidence that individuals may gain weight when their friends gain weight. These findings support the idea that the behavior of our associates and friends provides a context for setting standards for ourselves and that weight gain among others may justify relaxation in our own standards for fitness. Accordingly, if therapists can help patients identify others who have formed exercise teams, it may help establish some health contagion for the patient.

Also, we recommend helping the patient develop a broader vision of what his mood improvements may bring. The Valued Activities form provides four life areas—social activities, movies/theater/recreation, relationship activities, hobbies, volunteer activities, and work-related activities—that help define an individual's regular non-exercise activities. We recommend that at this early stage of treatment, patients are asked to consider what they will be doing when they meet their treatment goals. This provides patients with a vision for the sort of improvement they want and can also help them start establishing these behaviors, which will support the mood improvements they are achieving. The role of the therapist is to help elicit and define these activities and to encourage the sequential adoption of these goal activities as treatment progresses. The exercise intervention may provide the increased substrate by helping the patient decrease negative mood while improving energy and motivation. With this basic structure for broader goal attainment in place, therapists can then turn to providing the patient with a broader model of the change process brought about by exercise.

Chapter 2 of the workbook provides patients with information on how exercise may treat mood and anxiety disorders. This information has also been reviewed—at a more academic level—in Chapter 1 of this therapist guide. For discussion of the mechanism of treatment with patients, we recommend providing the following summary information.

Exercise may work by any of a number of mechanisms, and there is currently evidence that supports each of the following influences:

■ Exercise leads to changes in some of the same neurotransmitters targeted by antidepressant medications. For example, exercise stimulates the activity of serotonin, an important neurotransmitter for the regulation of emotion, and is the main neurotransmitter affected by medication such as Paxil®, Prozac®, Zoloft®, and Celexa®. So, one way of thinking about exercise effects is that with exercise you are driving important biological changes in your brain that can help with the management of mood and stress.

■ Exercise helps break self-perpetuating cycles that involve low activity or avoidance. Exercise may work in part because it returns the body to adaptive action. Also, as you learn to exercise independently of the way you feel, the meaning of your negative emotions will change. Sad or anxious feelings may start to become less overwhelming; this is because exercise is expected to increase your resilience to negative mood states. As you stay active despite low moods, these episodes of mood should last less time.

■ In addition to more direct effects on neurotransmitters and activity levels involved in the regulation of mood, exercise may also have indirect effects on mood through the normalization of sleep. Sleep problems have been implicated in either the onset or maintenance of both mood and anxiety disorders. With regular exercise, we have the expectation that your sleep quality will improve.

■ In addition to these effects on activity and rest, exercise may provide your body the moderation it needs to promote mood stability, while also breaking up periods of overthinking, worry, and rumination. Also, the beneficial effects of exercise on reducing feelings of stress may have importance for *prevention* of both mood and anxiety disorders.

■ It is also important to keep in mind, and make clear to the patient, those patterns that exercise is presumed not to treat. The patient workbook specifically reminds patients that encouragement to use exercise to help manage mood and anxiety disorders should not be taken as encouragement to ignore other treatment options. Likewise, it should be clarified that use of exercise to moderate stress is not a substitute for the use of good problem-solving skills, and that in the case of depression, suicidal ideation always deserves direct attention by a mental health professional.

Helping Patients Manage Motivational Issues

A central message of the patient workbook is that motivational barriers to exercise are predictable, understandable, and treatable. Prior to the exercise prescription and the patient's initial attempts to establish a pattern of regular exercise, it is important to help inoculate patients against specific motivational barriers and educate them about ways to circumvent motivational lapses. We recommend presentation of the following information:

■ Motivation is frequently assumed to be a stable inward trait that precedes behavior change and helps determine the success of your goals and intentions. This is not necessarily true. A strong motivation to change does not always precede useful behavior change. This is because the desire to do something often follows the successful completion of the behavior. It is by doing something one or more times that one can establish the inward desire (the motivation) to do it again. As such, we don't expect you to have a strong feeling that exercise is important. That feeling may well come *after* you have successfully altered your mood, anxiety, or stress through exercise.

■ The key is making new habits easy to start and maintain by manipulating your environment rather than hoping for motivation.

- The strategy is to make changes in your environment in order to make changes in your motivation. In short, rather than expecting yourself to feel like exercising, you should *arrange your environment* so that you will more naturally feel like exercising.

- Work to put yourself in the conditions where going to the gym or going running is a more natural thought. So, instead of focusing on getting yourself to the final outcome of being in the middle of exercise, *focus only on the next step* that will make it more likely that you will exercise. For example, from the position of being on the couch, the first goal is helping yourself take one step toward being ready for exercise, such as putting on your workout clothes. Figure 2.1 illustrates this process. The same figure is provided for the patient in the corresponding workbook.

Hard way to get yourself to exercise:

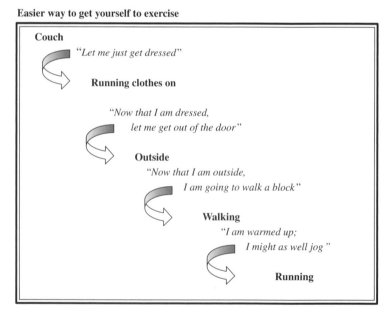

Figure 2.1

Setting the Stage for Exercise Success

The goal of this discussion is to help the patient think through ways in which he can change the situation (and how he is currently thinking and feeling) enough to make it more likely that he will exercise. For example, the patient workbook provides the following suggestions for behaviors to provide a chain between inaction and exercise:

- Change into your workout clothes.

- Decide to do 10 sit-ups on the floor or some brief stretching while you are deciding whether to exercise.

- Go to the bathroom and look at your eyes in the mirror and discuss with your reflection whether you want to exercise.

- Think of the good music you might listen to while exercising and go get your music player.

- Daydream about how it will feel when you are done exercising.

- Remember how good you felt when you exercised last.

- Call a friend and see if he wants to exercise.

- Get out your workbook and review a chapter.

- Get yourself a glass of ice water to prepare (hydrate) for exercise.

- Remind yourself that a bad mood is a reason to exercise, not a reason to skip exercise.

- Remind yourself that starting your exercise is often the most difficult part of your exercise routine; once you start, it will get easier.

In addition to chaining, interventions prior to the exercise prescription include inoculation against specific cognitions and motivational patterns that may be linked to exercise at specific times of the day. The role of the therapist is to provide patients with a vision of the type of motivational challenges that may arise as exercise is worked into the patient's schedule at different times of the day. For example, you may say something like the following:

> At the end of the session, I am going to assign you an activity schedule and ask you to write down your weekly schedule of activities and events

as they occur. With this completed exercise schedule in hand next session, you and I will be in a better position to talk about how exercise can best fit in your weekly schedule. If possible, I want you to schedule exercise around natural breaks in your day, keeping in mind the times of the day when exercise is likely to make you feel best. Also, because exercise typically involves a change of clothes and, in many cases, a shower afterwards, it is important to plan how these disruptions fall into your daily schedule. Before we get to your personal schedule, let's talk about some common patterns in exercise at different times of the day.

Some individuals select morning exercise as a way to start the day. Some advantages include the following:

- *Exercise is an excellent way to start the day.*

- *The exercise shower becomes the morning daily shower.*

- *Morning time may allow more optimal weather conditions.*

- *Early morning time is excellent "me time."*

- *All day you get to enjoy the sense of accomplishment of having already exercised.*

I would also like to get you to consider ways in which individuals derail their morning exercise efforts, so that you can be prepared to counter these common motivation-sapping thoughts.

By knowing the form and content of these thoughts, I believe you will be better able to "coach" yourself in relation to them. For example, you may say,

"Hey, I recognize this thought; this is one of those thoughts that leads me off track. What can be a more useful way for me to coach myself?" Typical morning negative thoughts that can sap motivation include the following:

- *I will skip my workout just this one time.*

- *It is too cold out of bed.*

- *It will be more valuable for my mood if I sleep in.*

- *Missing my workout once won't matter.*

Do you see how these thoughts can make it harder for you to exercise? (Allow discussion of this point, communicating the power this negative self-coaching can have on individuals.)

You will also want to review behavioral and cognitive patterns specific to avoidance of exercise at certain times of the day. For morning exercise, this involves review of the concept of the "awake mind." You may say the following:

Remember that you made your decision to exercise when you had an ***awake*** *mind the previous evening. Don't let any of the following thoughts have power to push you away from exercising (and these thoughts do have lots of power for a half-awake mind):*

- *I will just turn over in bed one more time before I get up.*

- *Staying in bed 10 more minutes won't matter.*

- *I am too tired to exercise well.*

- *I can always exercise this evening.*

Anticipating your reactions the night before your exercise may help you counter your arguments against starting exercise the next morning. Having these thoughts hit you in the morning may then even bring a knowing smile to your face and motivate you to get started.

You should also complete a similar review of afternoon and evening exercise. This can be done as a freeform discussion including the following points or as part of specific review of this information as presented in Chapter 3 of the patient workbook.

For exercise in the afternoon, cover the following advantages, barriers, and solutions:

- An exercise break is an excellent strategy for stress management and makes use of the sort of segmented day that is so popular in European countries (with an extended lunch and afternoon break before returning to work).

- With a fixed mid-day break for exercise, the workday can lose its marathon quality.

- There is the morning work routine, and then a break where the levels of stress are reduced.

- The body gets to be active, the mind gets to rest, and then one can return to the afternoon physically tired but mentally refreshed and ready to meet home, work, school, or personal goals.

One of the major challenges to getting out for the mid-day exercise break is the tendency to *one more thing* yourself away from exercise. Thoughts characterizing this "one more thing" way to sap your motivation include the following:

- I am working well; I will get just one more thing done.

- I am too busy. I better not take a break till later.

- If I don't finish this now, it will be too overwhelming later.

To counter "one more thing" thoughts, you may want to remind yourself:

- I am taking a break to exercise to have a fresh mind for my afternoon job demands.

- I know that I feel different after exercise; let me see what work feels like under those conditions.

- Management of my stress and mood is one way I am helping myself be more productive.

Likewise, for exercise in the evening, review the following benefits over exercise in the afternoon or morning:

- Evening exercise can be a terrific way to close out the day and prepare for an especially relaxed and enjoyable end to your day.

- Some people use evening exercise as a way to close out the work day and reduce stress prior to being with family or friends.

- Others may be able to incorporate a run into their commute home or use exercise and the post-exercise shower and change of clothes as their way to prepare for an enjoyable evening.

- Exercising approximately 3 hours before sleep is also excellent timing to help you have time to recover from exercise and take advantage of some of the natural sedating properties of a good workout.

One of the challenges of evening exercise is that you may need to cope with exercise avoidance due to fatigue from the day. Motivation-sapping thoughts include the following:

- I am too tired. I can just put it off until morning.

- It is about to get dark.

- It will be too cold.

Alternative self-coaching includes the following thoughts:

- If I exercise tonight, I think I will feel good and accomplished, and my mood and mental energy may be good in the morning.

- It is cold, but if I exercise I will feel good this evening and I really will enjoy a hot shower afterwards and sleep well.

For evening exercise, it is helpful to consider how you can exercise right after work or school. This can help reduce the loss of motivation for exercise that occurs once someone finally makes it home after a long day. A long day may make exercise especially rewarding and refreshing, but after returning home, going back out for exercise can be especially difficult. Even at this stage of preparing for exercise, it is helpful to have patients think about how to make exercise easier by managing the situational variables that either promote or act as a barrier to motivation.

Closing the Session

At the end of this session, the patient should recognize that the exercise prescription, although simple, requires effort and comes with definite challenges. What all this means is that the patient should be prepared to manage the challenges. In addition to reviewing with the patient the material covered during this session, the patient would benefit from reading Chapters 1 to 4 in the workbook prior to the next session, during which you will introduce the exercise prescription.

Chapter 3   *The Exercise Prescription*

(Corresponds to chapters 5 & 6 of the workbook)

Materials Needed

- Copy of patient workbook

- Selecting Activities Worksheet

- Formula for determining target heart rate

- Worksheet for Determining Initial Exercise Training Progression

- Daily Schedule Planner

- Exercise Planning Worksheet

- Exercise for Mood Log

Outline

- Introduce the parameters of the exercise prescription

- Help the patient select activities

- Introduce the recommended exercise dose

- Develop an exercise program progression schedule

- Introduce the components of an exercise session

- Introduce strategies for helping patients initiate the program

During this and subsequent sessions, you will work together with the patient to develop and fine-tune an aerobic exercise program that can help the patient manage depressed mood or anxiety. Successful implementation and maintenance of an exercise program may very well depend on how well the program fits the patient's preferences. As such, it is important to provide the patient with a sense of control derived by setting her own activity schedule. Accordingly, before prescribing the exercise dose, introduce the patient to the following three exercise parameters:

1. **Intensity**

   Intensity is most commonly guided by either the caloric cost of an activity or the heart rate associated with an activity (American College of Sports Medicine [ACSM], 2005). Caloric costs of activities can be expressed in metabolic equivalency tasks (METs), where 1 MET reflects the amount of energy expended sitting quietly at rest adjusted to body weight (1 MET = 3.5 ml oxygen consumed/kg of body weight/minute; ACSM, 2005). Activities associated with less than 3.0 METs (e.g., walking slowly, mowing the lawn) are considered light in intensity; activities of 3–5.9 METs (e.g., walking at 3–4 mph, swimming leisurely, doubles tennis) are moderate in intensity; and activities greater than 6 METs (e.g., jogging or running at >4.5 mph, rollerblading, bicycling on flat ground at >12 mph) are vigorous in intensity. An extensive list of activities with corresponding MET levels can be found at http://prevention.sph.sc.edu/tools/docs/documents_compendium.pdf.

   An easy alternative to setting exercise intensity is to measure the person's heart rate during an activity and express it as percentage of the age-adjusted maximum heart rate (HR_{max} = 220-age; see table). The ACSM (2005) classifies activities that yield a heart rate of less than 64% of HR_{max} as light, 64–76% of HR_{max} as moderate, and 77–93% of HR_{max} as vigorous.

Intensity	MET level	% HR_{max}
Light	<3.0	<63%
Moderate	3–5.9	64–76%
Vigorous	≥6	77–93%

Suggest to the patient that she purchase a heart rate monitor. These devices are relatively inexpensive and simple to use. Not only can they be used to determine whether the patient is receiving the recommended exercise dose, the immediate heart rate feedback that the patient receives during exercise can guide possible modifications to intensity.

2. **Duration**

Duration is usually expressed in minutes, where most exercise prescriptions involve durations between 20 and 60 min (depending on the intensity; ACSM, 2005).

3. **Frequency**

Frequency is expressed in number of training sessions per week.

Reviewing these exercise parameters will naturally lead to a discussion of reasonable activities for the patient. Walking or running is a popular choice because these activities are readily available. Nonetheless, you and your patient should consider other available alternative activities (refer the patient to the Selecting Activities Worksheet in Chapter 5 of the workbook).

Recommended Dose and Training Progression

The available evidence supports an exercise prescription for patients with mood or anxiety disorders consistent with the recent Department of Health and Human Services (DHHS) public health recommendation for aerobic exercise:

1) Moderate-intensity aerobic exercise for at least 150 min (2 hr and 30 min) each week

OR

2) Vigorous-intensity aerobic exercise for at least 75 min (1 hr and 15 min) each week.

Indeed, not only have most investigations of the efficacy of exercise for mood and anxiety disorders to date examined a dose that is roughly equivalent to the public health-recommended dose (Stathopoulou et al., 2006), this dose has also shown clear benefits for promoting and maintaining good physical health (U.S. Department of Health and Human Services, 2008). For the treatment of mood and anxiety disorders, the literature indicates that aerobic activity should be performed in bouts of at least 25 min on 3 to 5 days a week.

Consistent with the exercise prescription guidelines put forth by the ACSM (2005), emphasize the importance of gradually increasing activity over the course of a few weeks to reach the recommended dose. Here, the rationale is that early success (i.e., meeting established goals) and preventing risk of injury ultimately increase the likelihood of successfully adopting a physical activity habit. Figure 3.1 presents a possible schedule for training progression (ACSM, 2005). Although most patients should be able to get up to the recommended dose within a 4-week period, it is important to be flexible.

Together with the patient, you can determine the appropriate progression schedule to get the patient to the correct exercise dose. You may say:

I realize that the idea of increasing your activity level to meet the recommended dose may sound daunting. In order to make this a success experience for you, I recommend that you start slowly and gradually increase your activity level over the course of the next few

Week	Exercise intensity	Exercise duration	Exercise frequency
1	65% of HR_{max}	15 min	2 times per week
2	65–70% of HR_{max}	15–20 min	2–3 times per week
3	70–75% of HR_{max}	20–25 min	3–4 times per week
4	75–80% of HR_{max}	25–30 min	3–5 times per week

Figure 3.1

Sample Initial Exercise Training Progression

weeks. What do you believe is a good starting point for the next week? How would you like to change the following week to get closer to the recommended dose?

As you work with patients to get them up to the public health recommended dose, it is important to consider their preferences. Because there is no indication for a specific combination of frequency, duration, and intensity of sessions for the management of mood and anxiety disorders in general, you should remind patients that they can vary these parameters to meet their preferences. One exception to this general rule is that for the treatment of panic disorder, the patient should work up to a schedule that includes exercise at sufficient intensity to create the somatic symptoms of exertion (target heart rate of >76% of HR_{max}). Chapter 5 presents specific strategies for assisting patients with panic disorder during this initial phase of the program.

Formatting the Exercise Session

Recognizing that many patients presenting for treatment are sedentary and may have little experience with exercise (Galper, Trivedi, Barlow, Dunn, & Kampert, 2006), it is important that you spend some time educating the patient about the components of an exercise training session. The ASCM (2005) recommends that the training portion of the session (e.g., 25 min of running at 80% of HR_{max}; 30 min of walking at 65% of HR_{max}) be preceded by a warm-up period and followed by a cool-down period. You may use the following sample dialogue to review the components of an exercise session with the patient:

> *In order to decrease the risk of injuries, I recommend that you take some additional time for a warm-up and cool-down before and after each exercise session. If you go for a brisk walk or run, spend the first 10 to 15 minutes walking slowly and do some stretching activities. You should then slowly increase the intensity of your activity until you reach the target heart rate range. I realize that you may just want to sit down after you have finished your exercise. However, it is better for your body to continue to walk slowly for an additional 5 minutes, with some periodic stretching. A cool-down allows your body to gradually recover from the intense activity.*

You should expect a good proportion of patients with mood and anxiety problems to either be apprehensive about initiating exercise or otherwise express concern about being able to make a change in this health behavior and maintain this change over time. Chapters 4 and 5 of this guide discuss specific strategies that can help increase the success of this treatment program with patients suffering from depression and anxiety disorders. Here, we would like to point out some useful tactics for initiating exercise that can be used with all patients and should be introduced early on in the treatment.

1. Setting a Specific Schedule for the Week

Putting exercise on the calendar (e.g., the Daily Schedule Planner) is the first step. Use the Exercise Planning Worksheet in Chapter 5 of the workbook to help the patient to determine the exercise plan for the upcoming week. Encourage the patient to approach exercise much like other activities (work or social) that the patient has planned for that week.

2. Identifying and Addressing Potential Barriers

Recognizing that patients may experience difficulties complying with the set schedule, you and the patient should spend time identifying possible barriers to exercise and brainstorm some strategies to overcome them.

I realize that it may be difficult to motivate yourself to start to exercise, especially early in the program when you have not yet experienced the positive benefits of exercise. Being aware of barriers to exercise and developing possible solutions will help you become successful in making exercise part of your daily life. Let's take a look at the bottom of the Exercise Planning Worksheet in Chapter 5 of your workbook. What do you perceive as your barriers? What are some possible solutions to each of these barriers?

My exercise schedule for this week is as follows:			
Monday Activity: _Run_ Intensity: _65% HR_{max}_ Duration: _25 min_	**Tuesday** Activity: _____ Intensity: _____ Duration: _____	**Wednesday** Activity: _Run_ Intensity: _70% HR_{max}_ Duration: _30 min_	**Thursday** Activity: _____ Intensity: _____ Duration: _____
Friday Activity: _____ Intensity: _____ Duration: _____	**Saturday** Activity: _Run_ Intensity: _75% HR_{max}_ Duration: _40 min_	**Sunday** Activity: _____ Intensity: _____ Duration: _____	**SUMMARY** **Intensity:** _65–75%_ **Duration:** _25–40 min_ **Frequency:** _3_

Anticipated barriers	Possible solutions
1. Travel for work	1. Stay at a hotel that has exercise facilities
	2. Join a gym that has multiple locations in multiple cities
	3. Join the YMCA or YWCA
2. Lack of energy	1. Plan to exercise in the morning when I feel most energetic
	2. Remind myself that my energy increases with exercise
	3.

Figure 3.2

Example of Completed Exercise Planning Worksheet

Figure 3.2 shows a sample completed worksheet.

3. Exercise Clothing

Depending on your patient's experience with exercise, you may want to review what your patient is planning to wear during exercise. Attention should be placed on the appropriateness of the clothing to the weather, the level of perspiration expected, comfort, and foot support.

Preplanning what is to be worn can also serve as a useful behavioral chaining exercise—by preplanning clothing, you are removing a potential obstacle to the first exercise session ("I don't know what to wear . . . maybe I don't have the right clothes . . . this is too hard . . . I will start next week"). Also the selection of exercise clothes can act as either a motivator or a pleasant reward for good exercise habits. Keep in mind that helping your patient wear comfortable clothes and dress appropriately for the weather (with care toward protecting against being too hot or too cold, or layering to allow adaption during running, for example) can go a long way in increasing the joy of exercise.

4. Route Considerations

Especially early on in the exercise training program, planning a running/jogging/walking route beforehand may help your patient mentally prepare for the exercise session. Asking your patient where she will exercise and reviewing the characteristics of the situation (level of traffic, sidewalk quality, things to look at, distances, safety, etc.) can help make preparation for exercise more real and can help you troubleshoot potential barriers to a pleasant exercise session. Also, you may want to have your patient use distance markers (e.g., intersection, post office, and school) for walking or running exercise to help her break up her activity into smaller parts that are each characterized by a feeling state (e.g., hard, smooth, struggle, easy). For example, you may say:

> Starting your exercise may be easier if you have planned a route beforehand. The easiest perhaps is to start and end at your house. Or, if you prefer a park and you live close to it, you may consider completing your exercise there. One possibility is to map your run using a Web site like mapmyrun.com. As you plan your route, you should build in distance for the warm-up and cool-down period. I also recommend that you think of your route as consisting of several different sections—some are challenging and are likely to sap your motivation; others are easier and will make you feel good about exercise. For example, that first section after the warm-up to the traffic light about a mile from your house may always be the most challenging part of your run—you are still a bit stiff and your muscles may feel

tight. Once you get to the traffic light, you have warmed up and
hitting the pavement feels much better—you are feeling good. On your
way home, you will have to climb that hill—3 minutes of hard work
that are followed by an easier section—you will struggle for a while
but will be rewarded soon by a feeling of accomplishment.

5. Making Exercise More Entertaining

Listening to music or the radio during exercise (or watching television, if exercising at an equipped gym or home) can help make exercise more pleasurable. Some individuals use it as a primary context of exercise (e.g., "I get to watch my show as long as I am exercising" or "I want to listen to my radio program; I might as well exercise while I do it"). As part of the exercise prescription, review with the patient strategies for adding entertainment, including the cost and place to buy small radios with headphones (a fairly low cost investment) or the use of digital music devices (e.g., iPods). Do remind patients that care needs to be taken when wearing headphones to avoid dangerous situations; sounds of passing cars, bikes, and rollerbladers can be blocked by loud music, and so extra care (e.g., exercising with just one earphone in place) needs to be taken when exercising in busy areas. Also, help your patient consider whether initial exercise sessions will be conducted alone or with an exercise partner. The more explicit you make the preparation for exercise, the better you may help your patient achieve initial exercise success.

6. Using Exercise Logs

Tracking progress will help the patient stay on track. It is recommended that patients complete the Exercise for Mood Log in the workbook for the first six weeks of the program. Completing this log will make clear to patients their efforts and achievements as well as the impact of exercise on their mood. Be sure to review this log with the patient during subsequent sessions. If the log indicates that the patient has completed the planned exercise, you can reinforce the patient's efforts and help the patient recognize the benefits (*"you can see how exercise helps improve your mood"*). Alternatively, a log that indicates that the patient has difficulty adhering to the program should motivate you to provide additional coaching (e.g., identify barriers, brainstorm possible solutions).

Next Steps in the Exercise Prescription

After structuring the starting point in exercise and establishing a rate of increase up to the public health recommended dose, the role of the therapist is to help the patient modify and maintain her exercise program. Whether follow-up sessions are needed weekly or every other week should be decided in relation to the patient's schedule, level of motivation, as well as goals. Weekly sessions can be brief (e.g., for 15 min) or can be integrated as a brief portion of a psychotherapy or medication check session. For these sessions, strategies for tailoring exercise to depression are presented in Chapter 4 and strategies for adapting exercise to the treatment of stress, worry, and panic disorder are presented in Chapter 5. In all cases, the task for the therapist is to facilitate the patient to plan and then complete her scheduled dose of exercise. Chapter 6 is devoted to clinical strategies to aid this process relative to the expected motivational and situational barriers that arise in the lives of individuals.

Chapter 4 | *Exercise for Depressed Mood*

(Corresponds to chapters 7–9 of the workbook)

Materials Needed

- Copy of patient workbook
- Pleasant Events List
- Exercise Planning Worksheet
- List of Good Sleep Strategies
- Exercise for Mood Log

Outline

- Provide education on the nature of depression
- Introduce strategies for managing depressogenic thoughts
- Discuss ways of extending the exercise prescription to other mood-enhancing activities
- Monitor compliance and depressed mood

Targeting Depressed Mood With Exercise

Therapists can have confidence in the efficacy of exercise for depressed mood. As noted in Chapter 1 of this guide, numerous studies support the efficacy of exercise for major depression. We recommend you convey this sense of optimism about treatment to your patient as a counter to the many ways in which depression will sap your patient's motivation for action and expectations of change. In treating major depression, you will want to make sure that your patient sees low mood and poor motivation as a reason to exercise rather than a reason to remain inactive. To achieve this goal, the patient must see depression as a syndrome that involves negative thinking and impaired motivation and as a disorder that can be treated by action—specifically the action that is inherent to regular exercise. In addition, remind your patient that exercise can bring about change to mechanisms involving some of the same brain chemicals (neurotransmitters) that are targeted by antidepressant medication.

The sections that follow review ways to introduce your patient to depression as a syndrome and to provide him with some therapeutic inoculation against the negative thoughts that are likely to arise from depression. In addition to these strategies, use of a support network and other therapeutic activities is recommended for depressed patients.

Education on the Nature of Depression

Education on the nature of depression serves a number of functions. In particular, educating patients about the different aspects of depression (e.g., symptoms, cognitions, and behaviors) and the nature of their interaction will help take away the mystery of the experience of depression, can reduce self-criticism around the symptoms of depression (i.e., depression about depression), and can help mobilize self-directed efforts to resist self-perpetuating cycles in depression. Also, education about depression can serve as a mobilizing force in applying exercise interventions despite depressed mood. Education on the nature of depression should include at least the following elements:

Symptoms

Highlight for the patient the difference between depressed mood and clinical forms of depression such as major depressive disorder and dysthymia. You may use the following sample dialogue:

Almost everyone feels blue or sad from time to time. Major depressive disorder is present when these feelings of sad mood are experienced for

at least two weeks and are accompanied by a set of other symptoms
such as lack of interest, feelings of guilt, low energy, concentration
problems, disrupted appetite, agitation or difficulties moving, sleep
disruptions, and perhaps, suicidal thoughts.

Negative Thinking Patterns

Introduce to the patient the idea that depression involves a number
of self-perpetuating cycles that are characterized by thoughts of failure
and disappointment and negative expectations about the self, others,
and the future. Care should be taken to introduce the idea of "depression about depression," which is the notion that self-criticism about
the symptoms of depression ("I can't believe I stayed in bed all day.
I am a lousy person", "Look at me! I can't even concentrate anymore;
I don't deserve to feel better") maintains and extends the depression
(Teasdale, 1983, 1988). By cautioning the patient about this pattern
(*"I want you to be aware of how you treat yourself when you notice symptoms of depression"*) and emphasizing the way in which the patient forms
his negative thoughts during depressed moods, you can make clear to
the patient that he often experiences negative thoughts about himself,
others, and ongoing goals. It is important here to discuss and potentially
address the patient's negative thoughts as they relate to the exercise program. If the patient indicates that he has little hope that the exercise
program will help him manage his mood and achieve other goals, you
may say something like the following:

> *I am not surprised that you have these negative thoughts—again, they*
> *are characteristic of depression. I know that these thoughts can be*
> *strong, particularly when you feel as stressed or depressed as you do*
> *now. In fact, I would like you to expect that, while feeling depressed,*
> *you will have especially negative thoughts about yourself and negative*
> *expectations about the future. You may find yourself saying things like,*
> *"this won't work out," "look at me! I am different because I am not*
> *happy," "I am failing." These thoughts come to mind very easily*
> *because of the depression. You may also find yourself self-critical of the*
> *symptoms of depression. Things like getting mad at yourself because*
> *your concentration may be poor, or calling yourself names because you*

feel bad or unmotivated, only make the depression stronger.
When you are depressed, I want you to make sure that you speak
kindly to yourself and direct yourself toward useful tasks to help
with your depression. Exercise is one of those tasks, but I want you to
know that depression will interfere with your motivation to
exercise.

You are encouraged to introduce a framework for responding differently to negative thoughts. For this, you may adopt an essential feature of cognitive therapy: Having the patient treat his thoughts as "guesses" about the world rather than as facts. You may use the following sample dialogue with the patient:

Particularly now, when you are depressed, I would like you to listen in
on your thoughts and notice both the tone and contents. Rather than
assuming your thoughts are accurate, I would like you to treat your
thoughts as guesses about the world. Once you treat your thought as a
guess, I would then like you to ask yourself whether these thoughts are
on track and useful—do the thoughts coach you toward useful action
or do they just make you feel bad and sap your motivation? I also want
you to apply this process to thoughts about exercise. Depression will
introduce especially negative thoughts about exercise or your progress,
and I want you ready to coach yourself better, especially to remind you
that exercise can help you FEEL better.

As an alternative, you may also want to consider the use of a metaphor to describe the style of self-talk you want your patient to adopt while depressed. This coaching metaphor, used across a number of protocol-driven treatments in the Treatments*ThatWork*™ series by Oxford University Press, is reprinted here.

This is a story about little league baseball. I talk about little league
baseball because of the amazing parents and coaches involved. And by
"amazing" I don't mean "good." I mean "extreme."

But this story doesn't start with the coaches or the parents; it starts with
Johnny, who is a little league player in the outfield. His job is to catch
fly balls and return them to the infield players. On the day of our story,
Johnny is in the outfield and "crack!"—one of the players on the other
team hits a fly ball. The ball is coming to Johnny. Johnny raises his

glove. The ball is coming to him, coming to him . . . and it goes over his head. Johnny misses the ball, and the other team scores a run.

Now there are a number of ways a coach can respond to this situation. Let's take Coach A first. Coach A is the type of coach who will come out on the field and shout: "I can't believe you missed that ball! Anyone could have caught it! My dog could have caught it! You screw up like that again and you'll be sitting on the bench! That was lousy!" Coach A then storms off the field.

At this point, Johnny is standing in the outfield and, if he is at all similar to me, he is tense, tight, trying not to cry, and praying that another ball is not hit to him. If a ball does come to him, Johnny will probably miss it. After all, he is tense, tight, and may see four balls coming at him because of the tears in his eyes. If we are Johnny's parents, we may see more profound changes after the game. Johnny, who typically places his baseball glove on the mantel, now throws it under his bed. And before the next game, he may complain that his stomach hurts, that perhaps he should not go to the game. This is the scenario with Coach A.

Now let's go back to the original event and play it differently. Johnny has just missed the ball, and now Coach B comes out on the field. Coach B says: "Well, you missed that one. Here is what I want you to remember: high balls look like they are farther away than they really are. Also, it is much easier to run forward than to back-up. Because of this, I want you to prepare for the ball by taking a few extra steps backwards. As the ball gets closer, you can step into it if you need to. Also, try to catch it at chest level, so you can adjust your hand if you misjudge the ball. Let's see how you do next time." Coach B then leaves the field.

How does Johnny feel? Well, he is not happy. After all, he missed the ball—but there are a number of important differences from the way he felt with Coach A. He is not as tense or tight, and if a fly ball does come to him, he knows what to do differently to catch it. And because he does not have tears in his eyes, he may actually see the ball and catch it.

So, if we were the type of parent who wanted Johnny to make the Major Leagues, we would pick Coach B because he teaches Johnny how to be a more effective player. Johnny knows what to do differently, may catch more balls, and may excel in the game.

But if we didn't care whether Johnny made the Major Leagues—because baseball is a game, and one is supposed to be able to enjoy a game—then we would again pick Coach B. We would pick Coach B because we care whether Johnny enjoys the game. With Coach B, Johnny knows what to do differently; he is not tight, tense, and ready to cry; he may catch a few balls; and he may enjoy the game. He may also continue to place his glove on the mantel.

Now, while we may all select Coach B for Johnny, we rarely choose the voice of Coach B for the way we talk to ourselves. Think about your last mistake. Did you say, "I can't believe I did that! I am so stupid! What a jerk!"? These are "Coach A" thoughts, and they have many of the same effects on us as Coach A has on Johnny. These thoughts make us feel tense and tight, may make us feel like crying, and rarely help us do better in the future. Remember, even if you were only concerned about productivity (making the Major Leagues), you would still pick Coach B. And if you were concerned with enjoying life, with guiding yourself effectively for both joy and productivity, you certainly would pick Coach B.

During the next week, I would like you to listen to see how you are coaching yourself. If you hear Coach A, remember this story and see if you can replace "Coach A" thoughts with "Coach B" thoughts.

In addition to discussing and addressing motivation-sapping thoughts, you should emphasize the effects that exercise has on the negative thinking patterns characteristic of depression. You may say something like the following:

Exercise offers you the opportunity to have a rumination-free period. As you start running, you may notice that your mind slowly becomes quiet and that you start focusing your attention on other things, such as the people you see, the sky, the trees, and your music. As you continue, you find your mind returning to how you are when you're not depressed. I recommend that you remind yourself of this outcome as you are preparing for exercise and perhaps are battling motivation-sapping thoughts. Tell yourself that your exercise is a time when you have an opportunity to be in the moment, feeling whatever you feel during the run, and enjoying your music and the sights along your running route.

Extending the Exercise Prescription to Other Mood-Enhancing Activities

Many patients describe depression as going into "shutdown" mode. The reduced activity level that is characteristic of depression strengthens negative thoughts and at the same time reduces opportunities to restore mood. Emphasize the importance of breaking these maladaptive and affect-linked habits and encourage the patient to develop a series of mood-enhancing activities in addition to exercise. Using the workbook as a therapy aid, encourage the patient as follows.

To help provide you with a balanced lifestyle, exercise should be one part of a series of mood-enhancing activities. Help for this goal is provided in Chapter 7 of your workbook. After you have started on a regular exercise habit, see how you can extend your focus on mood-enhancing activities by adding in the pleasurable events that help promote a positive mood. Use the Pleasant Events List in Chapter 7, as well as a daily or weekly planner for scheduling these "buffering" events. We call them buffering events because they can help buffer the effects of a low mood or a stressful week. Having something to look forward to, even if you feel blue, and participating in these activities can have powerful effects on reducing depression. As exercise and activity increase as part of your exercise program, your desire for pleasant events may increase as well. We would like you to use the Daily Schedule Planner to better understand your average weekly schedule and to consider what changes you might like to make to provide more balance as well as the presence of regularly scheduled small activities or events to help you feel good. These events can be simple pleasant events—such as lunch with a friend, time for a hobby, a regular movie night, a special television show, etc.—as well as those

*events that give you a sense of achievement (gardening, cleaning off
your desk, finishing a project, etc.). As you take time to think about
and schedule regular involvement in pleasant activities, please consider
the list of potentially pleasurable activities in Chapter 7 of your
workbook. The value of this list is in encouraging you to consider a
range of regular activities that serve as a buffer against stress by
helping you engage in rewarding activities on a regular basis. Many
of these activities involve physical activity, and hence many of these
may be easier or more pleasurable to complete as you become
more fit.*

Monitoring Compliance and Depressed Mood

The previous discussion makes it clear that, particularly in the beginning when patients have not seen the benefits of exercise, it is important
for the therapist to monitor compliance and potential barriers to exercise. In these early sessions, you and the patient should spend time to
plan exercise sessions and discuss and problem-solve barriers to exercise using the Exercise Planning Worksheet. To increase compliance,
encourage the patient to be specific in his plan to exercise (i.e., determine specific dose, set a time of day). In addition to addressing negative
thoughts as barriers, probe for other common barriers such as time
("Let's see at what times during the day you have a 30-minute window"),
cost *("exercise does not have to be completed at a fitness center"),* or weather
*("try to find an indoor activity that is available at your local community
center").*

In addition to ongoing monitoring of suicidal ideation, we recommend that you regularly evaluate whether negative mood is shifting as
a function of exercise. The Exercise for Mood Log can be particularly
useful to illustrate that exercise has an immediate payoff. In order to
help the patient recognize the long-term benefits of exercise on mood
(and thereby enhance compliance with the exercise prescription), consider administering a depression inventory on a weekly basis. A short
self-report measure like the Quick Inventory of Depressive Symptomatology (QIDS; Rush et al., 2006; see appendix) can be used for this
purpose.

Applying Exercise to Bipolar Disorder

In addition to helping alleviate bipolar depression (using the same exercise interventions as for unipolar depression), exercise has a positive effect on other negative affective states often reported by bipolar patients, as well as effects on the physiological processes that are implicated in the maintenance of the illness. We recommend you make your patients aware of these effects prior to the initiation of the program (see Chapter 9 of the workbook) and over the course of the intervention, through monitoring, highlight the link between exercise, these processes, and improved functioning.

Monitor Negative Affective States

Exercise can reduce a number of negative affective states such as stress and anxiety, as well as irritability and anger (Daniel, Cropley, Fife-Schaw, 2006; Hassmen et al., 2000; Salmon, 2001), that characterize many bipolar patterns. Accordingly, exercise may help calm the emotions that can emerge as part of both poles (depression as well as mania) of bipolar illness and thereby help stabilize mood.

Monitor Sleep Patterns

Manic episodes are often precipitated by changes in sleep–wake habits (Malkoff-Schwartz et al., 2000). Accordingly, the outcome of bipolar illness can be improved by regulating the sleep–wake cycle (Ehlers et al., 1993). In addition to highlighting and monitoring the benefits of exercise for sleep quality and stability (Singh et al., 1997), review with the patient the following list of good sleep strategies (also included in Chapter 7 of the workbook).

Good Sleep Strategies

- Eliminate stress in the bedroom. Discussions about your life or family issues or evening work (e.g., paying bills and reading documents for work) should not take place in bed or in the bedroom. Save the bedroom for bed activities. Worry or work at a desk, not in bed.

■ Give yourself time to unwind before sleep. Make sure the last hour of activity before bedtime is relatively passive. Do not pay bills, do not work out life problems, and do not plan your workday just before going to bed; save these activities for earlier in the day when you are fresher. Before sleep, choose activities that are pleasant and take very little effort (e.g., television, reading, and talking). Go to bed only after you have had a chance to unwind and feel more like sleeping.

■ Use a regular daytime cycle to help with nighttime sleep. Avoid taking naps during the day. Use regular exercise (at least 3 hr before bedtime) to help increase sleep and induce normal fatigue. One way to establish a regular time for falling asleep is to have a regular time for waking up. Setting your alarm clock to a reasonable time and maintaining it throughout the week will eventually be helpful in stabilizing your sleep time.

■ Reduce caffeine use (certainly eliminate caffeine use after noon), and be wary of drinking alcohol or smoking within several hours of bedtime.

■ If you have sleep problems, be careful of trying too hard to get to sleep. Trying hard to get to sleep often has the opposite effect; it wakes a person up with feelings of frustration and anger. Instead, try to enjoy being in bed and resting, even if sleep does not come. Direct your attention to how comfortable you are in bed (how the pillow feels or how good it feels to lie down and stretch), how relaxed your muscles feel, and how you can let your thoughts drift. If sleep does not come in a reasonable time, get out of bed and do a calm activity in another room. Return to bed only when you feel sleepy.

■ Use muscle relaxation techniques in bed. Relaxation tapes may help you relax and feel even more comfortable in bed. Remember the goal is not to go to sleep but to become very comfortable in bed so that sleep comes naturally. Commercially available relaxation tapes may help with this process.

Monitor Weight

Several medications prescribed for the management of bipolar illness can lead to significant weight gain. Accordingly, as part of a longer-term strategy after the basic exercise habit has been established, you can introduce the exercise prescription as a strategy to help reduce some of the negative side effects of these established treatments for bipolar illness. Again, monitoring weight throughout treatment may reinforce compliance with the pharmacotherapy plus exercise intervention.

Monitor Daily Routine

As you work with the patient to create consistency in his daily routine, introduce exercise as an activity that is part of that routine, regardless of the mood state. Here, we suggest that you reinforce moderation and instruct the patient to resist urges to overexercise or skip exercise entirely. As part of this discussion, direct the patient to Chapter 7 of the workbook, which provides a range of activities that can serve as a buffer against stress and help establish a routine.

Chapter 5 | *Exercise for Stress, Worry, and Panic*

(Corresponds to chapter 10 of the workbook)

Materials Needed

- Copy of patient workbook

- Exercise Practice Log for Panic-Related Concerns

Outline

- Teach the patient how to recognize and defer worries

- Prepare to target fear of somatic arousal with exercise

- Fine-tune the exercise prescription for fears of anxiety sensations

- Monitor exercise avoidance and anxiety sensitivity

Using Exercise to Target Stress, Worry, and Panic

As outlined in Chapter 1, there is substantial empirical support for the use of exercise to target stress, worry, and panic. As a way to enhance outcome expectancies and increase motivation for the intervention, initial discussion with patients who suffer from anxiety or panic should focus on the effectiveness of the exercise prescription for achieving their goals. Particularly with patients who hold strong beliefs that their anxiety problems stem from a chemical imbalance, it is important to also share results of studies that indicate that the effect of exercise on neurotransmitters mimics that of many antidepressant medications commonly prescribed for anxiety disorders.

Although anxiety disorders differ significantly in their presentation, they share in common worry and/or hypervigilance, as well as the tendency to avoid. Many of the anxiety disorders, and particularly panic disorder and post-traumatic stress disorder (PTSD), are also characterized by fears of anxiety symptoms. The sections that follow discuss strategies to complement and fine-tune the exercise prescription to help target these core features of anxiety disorders.

Teaching Patients to Recognize and Defer Worries

To help patients better target their worry patterns for change, it is helpful to sensitize patients to the core features of these patterns. In particular, you will want to help the patient differentiate worry from problem solving. Problem solving is solution focused, where multiple potential solutions are reviewed relative to a well-defined topic for change—the problem. On the other hand, worry is a repetitive cognitive activity that focuses attention on potential problems without consideration of the probability of these problems or potential solutions. A core feature of worry is the "what if" thinking format that keeps the thoughts future- and catastrophe-oriented. Discuss this form of worrisome thoughts and help the patient to understand that worry does not generate useful action, but it does generate anxiety and physical discomfort. To illustrate this process, you may say something like the following:

> *As you get better at identifying worry, you will likely notice a wide range of "what if" thoughts. What if I get fired? What if my partner breaks up with me? What if the kids get sick? What if my friend is mad? What if the report is flawed? What if things get worse? And if you are worrying, you rarely stop to consider whether these "what if" outcomes are likely or whether you could cope with these outcomes should they occur. Most commonly, anxious individuals identify a "what if" thought, feel anxious, and then quickly jump to a different "what if" thought. Also, the more anxious you are, the more easily these worries about the future come to mind and the more believable the "what if" thoughts become. I want you to be aware of these patterns so that you are more able to identify worry as unproductive and work actively to defer worry thoughts.*

One role of exercise is to create a break from these unproductive thoughts. With vigorous-intensity aerobic exercise, many patients will report a reduction in anxious and ruminative thinking patterns, as well as relief from the feelings of stress and anxiety associated with such worry. Indeed, a break from worry thoughts can help patients regain perspective and shift their thinking style to generate potential solutions (in the case of worries about probable events or threats) or gain perspective that further consideration of an unlikely "what if" thought is unproductive and not worth the investment of time and anxiety. As such, one strategy for reducing worry is to defer it until after vigorous exercise. You may use the following sample dialogue to describe this strategy:

> *How do you get out of an unproductive cycle of worry and increasing anxiety? Creating breaks is one strategy. A break will often allow you to regain perspective on the situation. Ideally, you would use exercise as soon as you find yourself in a worry rut, but this is unlikely given your schedule. Instead, I would like you to defer worry whenever possible. After all, worrying is not problem solving, so there is no hurry to worry. In deferring worry, you may ask yourself: "Do I really need to think about this now, and is my thinking leading to solutions?" I recommend that you then set the goal of focusing on the present—events going on right now—so that you can stay free of "what if" thoughts until your exercise session later in the day. During the exercise, look forward to the way in which exertion can lead to a worry-free period and create a sense of calmness to help you stay worry-free for hours after exercise.*

Therapist Note

▪ *You will need to assess whether the patient needs problem-solving training to supplement worry interventions.* ▪

Preparing to Target Fear of Somatic Arousal With Exercise

A number of studies have implicated the tendency to fear anxiety and its related bodily sensations (i.e., anxiety sensitivity) in the onset and maintenance of panic disorder (cf. McNally, 2002) and other anxiety disorders (Schmidt, Zvolensky, & Maner, 2006). Individuals who have a high level of anxiety sensitivity respond to benign bodily sensations (e.g., racing heart, rapid breathing, and sweating) with fear because they are concerned that these sensations have harmful (physical, social, and mental) consequences. Growing evidence suggests that targeting anxiety sensitivity may be critical to overcoming panic disorder, and initial evidence suggests that reducing anxiety sensitivity may also improve outcomes for other anxiety disorders such as PTSD, as well as anxiety-related health behaviors such as smoking.

Because exercise induces arousal-related bodily sensations, individuals with a high level of anxiety sensitivity (e.g., patients with panic disorder) are likely to avoid exercise and may therefore be hesitant to initiate or maintain an exercise program without additional coaching from their therapist. Prior to providing the exercise prescription to patients with panic disorder, you should provide education on the role of fears of anxiety sensations in panic disorder and the efficacy of exposure to bodily sensations (through exercise) for overcoming anxiety sensitivity. Be sure to address the following points:

1. **Panic attacks are part of a natural alarm signal**

    A panic attack is an intense rush of fear accompanied by a host of symptoms, including dizziness, numbness, tingling, breathlessness, heart palpitations, sweating, and feelings of unreality. You can think of a panic attack as part of the natural fight-or-flight alarm that is designed to fire when we perceive danger. The symptoms of panic can be direct (e.g., rapid breathing) or indirect (light-headedness or chest pressure or pain resulting from rapid breathing) effects of this alarm reaction. At times of actual danger, attention is riveted to the source of danger. However, if the alarm reaction fires in the absence of danger, the alarm reaction symptoms become a focus of concern in their own right.

2. **Panic disorder is characterized by recurring false alarms**

    When anxiety and panic symptoms themselves become a focus of fear, recurrent panic attacks may emerge due to a fear of this escalation of anxiety. The alarm fires in response to the perceived danger of the symptoms or their feared consequences. Common fears among patients with panic disorder include the misinterpretation of anxiety and panic symptoms as signaling impending death ("Am I having a heart attack?" "Am I having a stroke?" "I am going to die"), impending loss of control ("I will faint" "I am going to have to run out of the room" "I can't find my way out or take care of the kids") or impending humiliation ("they are going to notice my symptoms and I will be humiliated" "they will think I'm crazy" "they will think I'm a fool"). These catastrophically negative interpretations of symptoms help cue the next panic attack by providing a false alarm for danger.

3. **Fear-of-fear cycle**

   Share with the patient the model (Figure 5.1) to illustrate that after initial panic attacks, a self-perpetuating pattern can develop to maintain and worsen the panic attacks. Here, it is important to explain why patients fear bodily sensations, even when they are not part of an anxiety reaction. You may say:

   After having learned to fear the alarm reaction, many patients start responding with fear to the bodily sensations that come along with panic, even if they occur outside the context of panic. That's

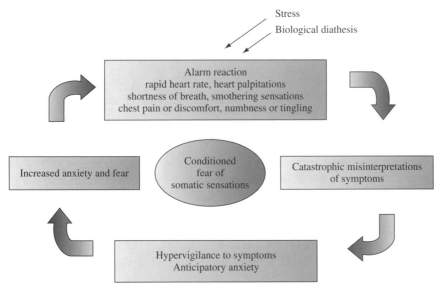

Figure 5.1

Cognitive-Behavioral Model of Panic Disorder

*why it is common for patients with panic disorder to fear
activities such as exercise or drinking coffee.*

4. **Exercise can provide interoceptive exposure to help extinguish
   fears of bodily sensations**

   Review with the patient the rationale for using exercise as a
   method to overcome the fears of somatic arousal, and thereby
   panic disorder.

   > *Exercise induces many of the feared bodily sensations that you
   > have been avoiding and thus gives you the opportunity to get used
   > to them again. It is that simple—repeated exposure results in
   > habituation. For example, consider a person who has developed
   > sleep problems after moving to a city that has 24-hr traffic. With
   > time, she will get used to the noises that first kept her up, allowing
   > her to return to her healthy sleep habit. Much like this example, it
   > is important that you use exercise to allow yourself to become
   > comfortable and embrace intense bodily sensations as natural and
   > expected. Once you learn this in the context of exercise, you have
   > built a memory that you can access when you are faced with
   > similar sensations that may arise due to anxiety and panic.*

   Present the patient with Figure 5.2 and discuss how exercise can help
   undo the fear-of-fear cycle and emphasize the importance of relaxing
   with sensations.

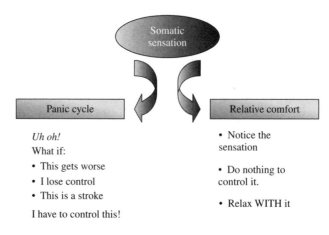

Figure 5.2

Reacting Differently to Panic Sensations

Having prepared the patient for targeting anxiety sensitivity, it should come as no surprise to the patient that the exercise prescriptions should be such that they can induce sufficient somatic arousal. Accordingly, an appropriate exercise prescription in this treatment plan should involve vigorous-intensity exercise (>76% of HR_{max}). In addition, we recommend that you encourage the patient to engage in active learning during the exercise session by completing the following steps:

1. **Prior to exercise**, instruct the patient to anticipate what sensations she is going to feel so that there are no surprises.

2. **During exercise**, instruct the patient to fully expect to experience these sensations. Instead of engaging in distraction strategies, remind the patient to focus on the sensations and see how comfortable she can get exercising while having the sensations.

3. **After exercise**, encourage the patient to draw her attention to the sensations she experienced during exercise and help her become confident that they are indeed safe. Using the Exercise Practice Log for Panic-Related Concerns in Chapter 10 of the workbook, have the patient record the sensations, rate their intensity on a 0–100 scale, and rate whether the experience of anxiety was associated with anxiety on the same scale. Then, ask the patient to examine whether the symptoms had any true adverse consequences relative to the fears of these sensations based on her experiences with panic.

Review these practice log sheets with the patient during subsequent sessions. Your role is to provide ongoing support while the patient uses exercise as a tool to become comfortable with once-frightening sensations of arousal. The goal is to then use this newfound comfort with sensations to end the fear-of-fear cycle. For example, therapists can direct patients to respond to anxiety and panic sensations just as they have learned to respond to similar sensations during exercise: Notice the sensations but do nothing to control them, and learn to relax with the sensations while continuing goal-directed activities.

In addition to helping patients address common barriers of exercise such as time, cost, or weather, you should evaluate whether the patient avoids exercise because of the fear of bodily sensations and provide additional coaching if necessary, particularly in the beginning of the program. In addition, we recommend that you regularly evaluate whether worry and anxiety sensitivity are improving with exercise. The Exercise for Mood Log can help reinforce the utility of exercise to reduce worry. Consider also administering the Anxiety Sensitivity Index (ASI; Reiss et al., 1986.) to illustrate the long-term effects of exercise for reducing the core fear underlying panic disorder.

Chapter 6   *Therapy Issues*

(Corresponds to chapters 3–11 of the workbook)

Materials Needed

- Copy of patient workbook
- Exercise Planning Worksheet
- Exercise for Mood Logs
- Monthly Exercise Log

Outline

- Help the patient develop a cognitive coaching style
- Work with the patient's barriers to regular exercise
- Prepare patient to deal with lapses
- Troubleshoot missed sessions
- Plan for variation
- Encourage monitoring exercise
- Terminate therapy

Therapist Note

■ *This chapter covers a range of issues to be addressed as they arise in therapy.* ■

The exercise prescription for mood improvement is relatively straightforward; the work for the therapist is to help patients successfully navigate motivational issues and other barriers to continuing this prescription. This chapter provides recommendations for helping patients develop a cognitive coaching style for both noticing and positively interpreting exercise experiences and working to eliminate barriers that arise during an exercise program.

Cognitive coaching refers to an adaptive style of self-talk that, in the case of this exercise program, is designed to direct attention to the most pleasurable aspects of exercise and exercise-related achievements during and after exercise. Use this coaching to also help the patient plan and initiate the next exercise session. Therapists can use both supportive discussions and Socratic questioning (questions designed to elicit the patient's own problem solving) to direct patients' attention to enjoyable aspects of their exercise experience as well the mood benefits they are achieving. Therapists can introduce these questions as part of providing additional information about effective self-coaching of their exercise experience. The dialogue between therapist (T) and patient (P) shown here exemplifies this process as the therapist assesses self-coaching style during and after exercise.

T: As you settle into your exercise program, I would like you to pay extra attention to how you are talking to yourself about your experience of exercise. Your motivation for exercise, and the degree to which you enjoy your exercise and post-exercise experience, may depend on how you direct your attention and how you coach yourself. For example, I want to make sure you are paying attention to the achievements you have made so far in adopting an exercise program. You have been exercising for 3 weeks so far and have succeeded in exercising 2–3 times per week. Have you commended yourself for these efforts?

P: Well, not really. I mean I missed two exercise sessions.

T: You did miss two sessions, but you made seven sessions. This effort deserves some notice!

P: I guess I have done OK.

T: I want you to be careful about how little credit you give yourself. If you heard that a friend started an exercise program and made seven of nine scheduled sessions, what would you say?

P: I guess I would say "good job," especially if they are just starting out . . . . like I am.

T: Good point—someone starting out with a new program deserves encouragement. And since you are the coach of yourself in this effort, it will be important for you to commend yourself for your efforts.

P: Yeah I guess so.

T: So let me hear it. Have you been on track—do you deserve a "good job"?

P: Yeah. Good job for me [smiles].

T: Nice. [pause] And while we are on the topic of coaching yourself, have you noticed what you tend to think about during exercise?

P: Oh yeah, I noticed that sometimes when I run I tend to count my breaths. It gets really tedious.

T: I bet. If you find that you are counting your breaths, what might be more fun to direct your attention toward?

P: I guess what is going on. In fact, I was running alongside a park the other day, and I noticed this tree that was changing colors. It was beautiful, and I noticed that I don't often pay attention to that sort of thing in the city. Sometimes my wife and I will drive out in the country to see the leaves, but I don't even notice them very well when they are on a tree just down the block. But on my run, I did happen to notice the colors.

T: It sounds like you have one solution to counting. If you notice that your attention has fallen to something boring on your run, you can redirect yourself to see if there is anything interesting to look at along the way.

P: Yeah.

T: And how about after your runs. How do you tend to feel?

P: You know I feel tired, but I usually feel good. I am not sure I am getting much of a mood lift in general, but after the runs I feel peaceful-like. I feel tired but good.

T: I like that phrase, "tired but good." I think the phrase captures a reality about a type of mood shift that happens from exercise. Exercise does make you physically tired but emotionally refreshed. I think "tired but good" captures that shift in mood.

P: Yeah, it is kind of neat to feel that. I usually just feel tired, or tired and cranky, at the end of the day.

T: As part of coaching yourself effectively around your new exercise habit, I want you to make sure to reflect on this "tired but good" feeling and remind yourself that you are changing your mood with exercise. You have further to go in the exercise program before we expect bigger changes in mood, but if you attend to, remind yourself about, and make sure to enjoy the mood changes you have had so far, it will help you maintain your motivation for the next exercise session.

P: That makes sense; sounds good!

Questions to consider for helping patients reflect on self-coaching before, during, and after exercise include:

- *What do you find helps the most to get you involved in exercise (particularly on days when your motivation is lower)?*

- *During exercise, to what do you find you are paying attention?*

- *What have been particularly positive moments during exercise; that is, do you remember any moments during exercise when you noticed feelings of well-being?*

- *At the conclusion of exercise (when you have finished doing what you set out to do) how do you feel? What do you say to yourself about your experience?*

- *What mood changes have you noticed from exercise thus far?*

- *What are ways in which you can better coach yourself around exercise—things you can say before, during, or after exercise?*

- *Do you find you have more energy or sleep better due to exercise?*

- *Has your sense of the seasons or your town or city changed because exercise gets you outside?*

- *How do you evaluate a day that involved exercise relative to a day that did not involve exercise? How do you feel about yourself and your accomplishments on these days?*

- *Have you developed new friendships because of exercise?*

Working With Barriers

During initial follow-up sessions, the role of the therapist is to work with barriers to the regular adoption of exercise. These barriers include both situational and motivational issues that may arise. For situational issues, practical problem solving is the prominent strategy to try to find an exercise schedule that is easy to adopt and maintain. Consider the following examples of typical barriers to exercise.

Work or Home Demands

Difficult and long work weeks can be a challenge to any exercise program. With extra effort going into work, many individuals will feel unable to put in additional effort for exercise. In addition to helping patients consider the ways in which exercise can have stress-reducing effects—and may play a role in enhancing attention and productivity at work—during such weeks, the fallback role for the therapist is to discuss ways for individuals to find time for at least minimal exercise (during the worst weeks, the goal may not be to hit the public health recommended dose of exercise but to maintain the general exercise habit to avoid a lapse). As such, even minimal exercise (sit-ups in the morning before work, a brief walk during the lunch hour, a walk with the family in the evening) can help keep the broader exercise habit going. For child care responsibilities, discuss with patients the degree to which children can be incorporated in exercise sessions. Jogging strollers can be an excellent way to provide talking time between parents and children (if the stroller does not put the child asleep), while also maintaining regular exercise.

Weather Challenges

Identification of indoor walking or running options can help patients continue exercise during inclement weather. Helping patients consider the use of local shopping malls (for walking) or gyms with treadmills or tracks for running can help keep patients on track during challenging seasons. In addition, encourage patients to consider how best to enjoy outdoor exercise despite the weather. Indeed, outdoor walking or running can help patients more enjoyably experience the changes in the seasons and reduce the degree to which weather traps individuals indoors. For example, with appropriate warm clothing (including hat and gloves), running during or after snowfall can be a wonderful experience—the white expanse, beauty of falling snow or frozen rivers, and the sound of the crunch of the snow with each step all add to the experience. Moreover, there is nothing quite like the warm shower and feelings of well-being that happen after a run in the rain or snow. Part of the role of the therapist is to discuss and help patients develop a vision for enjoying these aspects of outdoor exercise. Encouraging the patient to exercise outdoors despite weather challenges and to monitor his enjoyment of these experiences and any associated mood effects can help the patient develop stronger exercise habits that can last over the long term.

Injuries or Soreness

The goal of starting exercise in a stepwise fashion is to reduce the likelihood of injury or muscle pain. Nonetheless, injuries may occur (ankle twists, knee pain, falls, etc.), and helping a patient plan exercise in relation to these injuries is important. Medical evaluation of any injury or chronic or recurrent pain is the default recommendation. The role of the therapist is to help the patient come up with a plan for days off any exercise that aggravates his current condition and to provide information on whether substitute exercises are available. For example, for leg injuries, swimming or light weightlifting may provide useful substitutes for keeping an exercise program alive during a recovery period.

Motivational Issues

Management of self-coaching is important in maintaining early exercise efforts. At the early stages of establishing an exercise routine, the role of the therapist is to help patients identify any cognitive coaching patterns that help or hurt an exercise program and adopt those that help. Consider the following examples of negative thoughts and the cognitive coaching strategies used to alter these thoughts.

Negative thought	Coaching strategy
I am too busy; I will skip exercise just today.	Keeping a regular pattern of activity will probably help my efficiency and focus. Let's see how I do later today after exercising.
I feel bad today. Why bother?	This is exactly the mood state where exercise may give me energy and motivation.
I can skip today. I will just exercise tomorrow.	I need to be careful about skipping. When I exercise, I feel better, and if I keep the habit going, it will be easier to exercise later this week as well.

Dealing With Lapses

Therapists can play a useful role in helping patients develop a self-coaching style that supports exercise over the long term. When exercise has been useful in shifting mood, therapists will want to continue to help patients see the link between regular exercise and these benefits. Also, it is important to prepare patients for inevitable lapses in their exercise program, paying attention to preventing a temporary lapse from becoming a relapse to non-exercise. To do this, we recommend early discussions of responses to missed exercise sessions. For example, you may say something like the following:

It is natural to miss sessions of exercise, and perhaps the most important aspect of establishing a longer-term exercise habit is becoming good at getting yourself right back to an exercise routine after one or more missed sessions. It is important to remember that the quicker you get yourself back to exercise, the better you retain your level of fitness. Also, I want you to be particularly wary of the bad coaching that can happen after a missed session. This bad coaching (doom saying) takes a simple miss and translates it into a prescription for exercise failure. Such negative coaching includes the following thoughts:

- *I missed my exercise. I knew I could not stay with it.*

- *Regular exercise is just too hard. Why bother?*

- *I wrecked my benefits already. There is no point in continuing.*

- *I missed exercise all this week. I might as well just give up.*

Alternative and useful coaching for missed sessions includes:

- *It is a challenge to keep a perfect exercise schedule. There is no reason to beat myself up. I just need to get back on track with even a short exercise session.*

- *Making sure I exercise tomorrow will make it easier to get back to my full routine next week.*

- *I am doing this for my mood; not feeling like exercising is not a reason to miss.*

- *I like feeling in shape, and if I exercise later today, I get to keep and extend this feeling.*

- *I have to remember to exercise first, and expect to feel like exercising only after I am back on track.*

Chapter 5 of the workbook helps direct patients to the Exercise Planning Worksheet to work on barriers to exercise and the importance of tracking, noticing, and enjoying the mood benefits that exercise brings.

Troubleshooting Missed Sessions

An additional role for the therapist is to aid the patient's problem solving by helping him complete a functional analysis of the events leading up to a missed session, including the self-coaching strategies used by the patient. During this process, keep a resilient and curious attitude—showing interest in the patterns that led to the current lapse in exercise. In completing an analysis of the chain of events leading to missed exercise, you will want to assess (a) the situations in which the misses occur (evaluating the time of day, day of the week, presence of others, changes in job or home demands, or other stressors), and (b) immediate situational cues (did the patient consider exercise while standing or sitting, with the television on or off, with people home or not, etc.). Also review the characteristics of exercise leading up to the lapse by asking the following questions:

■ *How did you feel during your last exercise?*

■ *Do you remember what you were thinking at the time?*

■ *What did you tend to say to yourself after the exercise?*

■ *What might you say to yourself next time your motivation is low?*

Planning for Variation

As is noted in the patient workbook, the key to maintaining a strong exercise habit over time is variation. Variations include changes not only in the exercise to be completed, but also in what accompanies exercise—the clothes, the music, the friends, the time of day, the route, etc. In addition to assigning Chapter 11 of the workbook, you may want to consider discussing with the patient variations in the following parameters:

■ Changes in music or changing music for radio programs or books on tape.

■ Changing the exercise locale (trying a new gym, changing a running route, inviting along a new exercise partner, shifting exercise to new days/hours of the week).

■ Changing exercise activity (e.g., sign-up as a member for a team participating in a community league).

■ Using exercise as tourism (e.g., driving to a new locale for a sightseeing run).

- Buying new exercise clothes or rotating valued t-shirts across exercise outings.

- Setting new exercise goals (times, strength, etc.)

- Using competition (signing up for races, fun runs, or tournaments).

- Considering new longer-term goals (body shaping, weight reduction, energy levels, etc.)

- Use of classes for new skills (rock climbing, wind surfing, biking, etc.).

Monitoring Exercise

Throughout the early stages of an exercise program, regular monitoring of exercise should be encouraged. Moreover, if monitoring is assigned, it is crucial to complete a hands-on review of the patient's completed Exercise for Mood Logs to support continued involvement. Continued use of the logs is encouraged. However, once your patient has established a strong exercise habit, these logs will lose some of their usefulness. Instead, you may recommend that your patient use the Monthly Exercise Log in Chapter 11 of the workbook to coach himself toward new exercise goals. In addition, you may suggest the availability of free services like MapMyRun (http://www.mapmyrun.com) or FitLink (http://www.fitlink.com) to keep track of other health habits (e.g., sleep and nutrition) online.

Terminating Therapy

Review the patient's progress toward his goals and congratulate him on his accomplishments. Encourage him to continue with the program on his own, using the workbook as a resource. Inquire if the patient has any concerns about terminating therapy and address these as needed. Booster sessions might also be scheduled.

Quick Inventory of Depressive Symptomatology (Clinician-Rated) (QIDS-C)

Quick Inventory of Depressive Symptomatology (Clinician-Rated) (QIDS-C)

Name: _____ Today's date: _____

Please circle one response to each item that best describes the patient for the last seven days.

1. Sleep-onset insomnia:

    0   Never takes longer than 30 minutes to fall asleep.
    1   Takes at least 30 minutes to fall asleep less than half the time.
    2   Takes at least 30 minutes to fall asleep more than half the time.
    3   Takes more than 60 minutes to fall asleep more than half the time.

2. Mid-nocturnal insomnia:

    0   Does not wake up at night.
    1   Restless, light sleep with few awakenings.
    2   Wakes up at least once a night, but goes back to sleep easily.
    3   Awakens more than once a night and stays awake for 20 minutes or more, more than half the time.

3. Early morning insomnia:

    0   Less than half the time, awakens no more than 30 minutes before necessary.
    1   More than half the time, awakens more than 30 minutes before need be.
    2   Awakens at least one hour before need be more than half the time.
    3   Awakens at least two hours before need be more than half the time.

4. Hypersomnia:

    0   Sleeps no longer than 7–8 hours/night, without naps.
    1   Sleeps no longer than 10 hours in a 24-hour period (include naps).
    2   Sleeps no longer than 12 hours in a 24-hour period (include naps).
    3   Sleeps longer than 12 hours in a 24-hour period (include naps).

5. Mood (sad):

    0   Does not feel sad.
    1   Feels sad less than half the time.
    2   Feels sad more than half the time.
    3   Feels intensely sad virtually all the time.

6. Appetite (decreased):

    0   No change from usual appetite.
    1   Eats somewhat less often and/or lesser amounts than usual.
    2   Eats much less than usual and only with personal effort.
    3   Eats rarely within a 24-hour period and only with extreme personal effort or with persuasion by others.

7. Appetite (increased):

    0   No change from usual appetite.
    1   More frequently feels a need to eat than usual.
    2   Regularly eats more often and/or greater amounts than usual.
    3   Feels driven to overeat at and between meals.

8. Weight (decrease) within the last two weeks:

    0   Has experienced no weight change.
    1   Feels as if some slight weight loss has occurred.
    2   Has lost 2 pounds or more.
    3   Has lost 5 pounds or more.

9. Weight (increase) within the last two weeks:

    0   Has experienced no weight change.
    1   Feels as if some slight weight gain has occurred.
    1   Has gained 2 pounds or more.
    2   Has gained 5 pounds or more.

Enter the highest score on any one of the four sleep items (1–4 above) _____	**Enter the highest score on any one of the four appetite/weight-change items (6–9 above)** _____

10. Concentration/decision making:

- o No change in usual capacity to concentrate and decide.
- 1 Occasionally feels indecisive or notes that attention often wanders.
- 2 Most of the time struggles to focus attention or make decisions.
- 3 Cannot concentrate well enough to read or cannot make even minor decisions.

11. Outlook (self):

- o Sees self as equally worthwhile and deserving as others.
- 1 Is more self-blaming than usual.
- 2 Largely believes that he/she causes problems for others.
- 3 Ruminates over major and minor defects in self.

12. Suicidal ideation:

- o Does not think of suicide or death.
- 1 Feels life is empty or is not worth living.
- 2 Thinks of suicide/death several times a week for several minutes.
- 3 Thinks of suicide/death several times a day in depth, or has made specific plans, or has attempted suicide.

13. Involvement:

- o No change from usual level of interest in other people and activities.
- 1 Notices a reduction in former interests/activities.
- 2 Finds only one or two former interests remain.
- 3 Has virtually no interest in formerly pursued activities.

Total score: _____ (Range 0–27)

14. Energy/fatiguability:

- o No change in usual level of energy.
- 1 Tires more easily than usual.
- 2 Makes significant personal effort to initiate or maintain usual daily activities.
- 3 Unable to carry out most of the usual daily activities due to lack of energy.

15. Psychomotor slowing:

- o Normal speed of thinking, gesturing, and speaking.
- 1 Patient notes slowed thinking, and voice modulation is reduced.
- 2 Takes several seconds to respond to most questions; reports slowed thinking.
- 3 Is largely unresponsive to most questions without strong encouragement.

16. Psychomotor agitation:

- o No increased speed or disorganization in thinking or gesturing.
- 1 Fidgets, wrings hands, and shifts positions often.
- 2 Describes impulse to move about and displays motor restlessness.
- 3 Unable to stay seated. Paces about with or without permission.

> **Enter the highest score on either of the two psychomotor items (15 or 16 above)**
> _____

References

American College of Sports Medicine. (2005). *ACSM's guidelines for exercise testing and prescription* (6th ed.). Philadelphia, PA: Lippincott Williams, & Wilkins.

Bishop, F. L., Yardley, L., & Lewith, G. T. (2007). A systematic review of beliefs involved in the use of complementary and alternative medicine. *Journal of Health Psychology, 12*, 851–867.

Bosscher, R. J. (1993). Running and mixed physical exercise with depressed psychiatric patients. *International Journal of Sport Psychology, 24*, 170–184.

Broocks, A., Bandelow, B., Pekrun, G., George, A., Meyer, T., Bartman, U., et al. (1998). Comparison of aerobic exercise, clomipramine, and placebo in the treatment of panic disorder. *American Journal of Psychiatry, 155*, 603–609.

Broman-Fulks, J. J., Berman, M. E., Rabian, B., & Webster, M. J. (2004). Effects of aerobic exercise on anxiety sensitivity. *Behaviour Research and Therapy, 42*, 125–136.

Broman-Fulks, J. J., & Storey, K. M. (2008). Evaluation of a brief aerobic exercise intervention for high anxiety sensitivity. *Anxiety, Stress & Coping: An International Journal, 21*, 117–128.

Brown, R. A., Abrantes, A. M., Strong, D. R., Mancebo, M. C., Menard, J., Rasmussen, S. A., et al. (2007). A pilot study of moderate-intensity aerobic exercise for obsessive compulsive disorder. *Journal of Nervous and Mental Disease, 195*, 514–520.

Bruce, S. E., Yonkers, K. A., Otto, M. W., Eisen, J. L., Weisberg, R. B., Pagano, M., et al. (2005). Influence of psychiatric comorbidity on recovery and recurrence in generalized anxiety disorder, social phobia, and panic disorder: A 12-year prospective study. *American Journal of Psychiatry, 162*, 1179–1187.

Camacho, T. C., Roberts, R. E., Lazarus, N. B., Kaplan, G. A., & Cohen, R. D. (1991). Physical activity and depression: Evidence from the Alameda county study. *American Journal of Epidemiology, 134*(2), 220–231.

Casper, R. C., Katz, M. M., Bowden, C. L., Davis, J. M., Koslow, S. H., & Hanin, I. (1994). The pattern of physical symptom changes in major depressive disorder following treatment with amitriptyline or imipramine. *Journal of Affective Disorders, 31*(3), 151–164.

Chaouloff, F. (1997). Effects of acute physical exercise on central serotonergic systems. *Medicine & Science in Sports & Exercise, 29*(1), 58–62.

Christakis, N. A., & Fowler, J. H. (2007, July 26). The spread of obesity in a large social network over 32 years. *New England Journal of Medicine, 357*(4), 370–379.

Cox, B. J., Enns, M. W., Freeman, P., & Walker, J. R. (2001). Anxiety sensitivity and major depression: Examination of affective state dependence. *Behaviour Research and Therapy, 39*(11), 1349–1356.

Craft, L. L., & Landers, D. M. (1998). The effects of exercise on clinical depression and depression resulting from mental illness: A metaregression analysis. *Journal of Sport & Exercise Psychology, 20,* 339–357.

Daniel, J. Z., Cropley, M., & Fife-Schaw, C. (2006, August). The effect of exercise in reducing desire to smoke and cigarette withdrawal symptoms is not caused by distraction. *Addiction, 101*(8), 1187–1192.

DeRubeis, R. J., Gelfand, L. A., Tang, T. Z., & Simons, A. D. (1999). Medications versus cognitive behavior therapy for severely depressed outpatients: Mega-analysis of four randomized comparisons. *American Journal of Psychiatry, 156*(7), 1007–1013.

Dey, S., Singh, R. H., & Dey, P. K. (1992). Exercise training: Significance of regional alterations in serotonin metabolism of rat brain in relation to antidepressant effect of exercise. *Physiology and Behavior, 52,* 1095–1099.

Dishman, R. K. (1997). Brain monoamines, exercise, and behavioural stress: Animal models. *Medicine and Science in Sports and Exercise, 29,* 63–74.

Dishman, R. K., Heath, G. W., & Washburn, R. (2004). *Physical activity epidemiology.* Champaign, IL: Human Kinetics.

Doyne, E. J., Ossip-Klein, D. J., Bowman, E. D., Osborn, K. M., McDougall-Wilson, I. B., et al. (1987). Running versus weight lifting in the treatment of depression. *Journal of Consulting and Clinical Psychology, 55*(5), 748–754.

Driver, H. S., & Taylor, S. R. (2000). Exercise and sleep. *Sleep Medicine Reviews, 4*(4), 387–402.

Dunn, A. L., Reigle, T. G., Youngstedt, S. D., Armstrong, R. B., & Dishman, R. K. (1996). Brain norepinephrine and metabolites after treadmill training and wheel running in rats. *Medicine and Science in Sports and Exercise, 28,* 204–209.

Dunn, A. L., Trivedi, M. H., Kampert, J. B., Clark, C. G., & Chambliss, H. O. (2005). Exercise treatment for depression: Efficacy and dose response. *American Journal of Preventive Medicine, 28,* 1–8.

Eaton, W. W., Shao, H., Nestadt, G., Lee, H. B., Bienvenu, O. J., & Zandi, P. (2008). Population-based study of first onset and chronicity in major depressive disorder. *Archives of General Psychiatry, 65,* 513–520.

Ehlers, C. L., Frank, E., & Kupfer, D. J. (1988). Social zeitgebers and biological rhythms. *Archives of General Psychiatry, 45*(10), 948–952.

Ehlers, C. L., Kupfer, D. J., Frank, E., & Monk, T. H. (1993). Biological rhythms and depression: The role of zeitgebers and zeitstorers. *Depression, 1,* 285–293.

Eisenberg, D. M., Davis, R. B., Ettner, S. L., Appel, S., Wilkey, S., Van Rompay, M., et al. (1998, November 11). Trends in alternative medicine use in the United States, 1990–1997: Results of a follow-up national survey. *Journal of the American Medical Association, 280*(18), 1569–1575.

Farmer, M. E., Locke, B. Z., Moscicki, E. K. D. A. L., Larson, D. B., & Radloff, L. S. (1998). Physical activity and depressive symptoms: The NHANES I epidemiologic follow-up study. *American Journal of Epidemiology, 128,* 1340–1351.

Frank, E., Hlastala, S., Ritenour, A., Houck, P., Tu, X., Monk, T., et al. (1997). Inducing lifestyle regularity in recovering bipolar disorder patients: Results from the maintenance therapies in bipolar disorder protocol. *Biological Psychiatry, 41,* 1165–1173.

Galper, D. I., Trivedi, M. H., Barlow, C. E., Dunn, A. L., & Kampert, J. B. (2006, January). Inverse association between physical inactivity and mental health in men and women. *Medicine & Science in Sports & Exercise, 38*(1), 173–178.

Goodwin, R. D. (2003). Association between physical activity and mental disorders among adults in the United States. *Preventive Medicine, 36,* 698–703.

Greenberg, P. E., Sisitsky, T., Kessler, R. C., Finkelstein, S. N., Berndt, E. R., Davidson, J. R., Ballenger, J. C., & Fyer, A. J. (1999, July). The economic burden of anxiety disorders in the 1990s. *Journal of Clinical Psychiatry, 60*(7), 427–435.

Hassmen, P., Koivula, N., & Uutela, A. (2000). Physical exercise and psychological well-being: a population study in Finland. *Preventive Medicine, 30*, 17–25.

Hofmann, S. G., & Smits, J. A. (2008). Cognitive-behavioral therapy for adult anxiety disorders: A meta-analysis of randomized placebo-controlled trials. *Journal of Clinical Psychiatry, 69*(4), 621–632.

Hopko, D. R., Lejuez, C. W., Ruggiero, K. J., & Eifert, G. H. (2003). Contemporary behavioral activation treatments for depression: Procedures principles and progress. *Clinical Psychology Review, 23*, 699–717.

Jacobson, N. S., Martell, C. R., & Dimidjian, S. (2001). Behavioral activation treatment for depression: Returning to contextual roots. *Clinical Psychology: Science and Practice, 8*(3), 255–270.

Judd, L. L., Akiskal, H. S., Schettler, P. J., Coryell, W., Endicott, J., Maser, J. D., et al. (2003, March). A prospective investigation of the natural history of the long-term weekly symptomatic status of bipolar II disorder. *Archives of General Psychiatry, 60*(3), 261–269.

Judd, L. L., Akiskal, H. S., Schettler, P. J., Endicott, J., Maser, J., Solomon, D. A., et al. (2002, June). The long-term natural history of the weekly symptomatic status of bipolar I disorder. *Archives of General Psychiatry, 59*(6), 530–537.

Kessler, R. C., Berglund, P., Demler, O., Jin, R., Merikangas, K. R., & Walters, E. E. (2005). Lifetime prevalence and age-of-onset distributions of DSM-IV disorders in the national comorbidity survey replication. *Archives of General Psychiatry, 62*(6), 593–602.

Kessler, R. C., Chiu, W. T., Demler, O., Merikangas, K. R., & Walters, E. E. (2005, June). Prevalence, severity, and comorbidity of 12-month DSM-IV disorders in the national comorbidity survey replication. *Archives of General Psychiatry, 62*(6), 617–627.

Kessler, R. C., Soukup, J., Davis, R. B., Foster, D. F., Wilkey, S. A., Van Rompay, M. I., et al. (2001). The use of complementary and alternative therapies to treat anxiety and depression in the United States. *American Journal of Psychiatry, 158*(2), 289–294.

Klein, M. H., Greist, J. H., Gurman, A. S., Neimeyer, R. A., Lesser, D. P., Bushnell, N. J., et al. (1985). A comparative outcome study group psychotherapy vs. exercise treatments for depression. *International Journal of Mental Health, 13*, 148–177.

Kubitz, K. A., Landers, D. M., Petruzzello, S. J., & Han, M. (1996). The effects of acute and chronic exercise on sleep: A meta-analytic review. *Sports Medicine, 21,* 277–291.

Lydiard, R. B., Brawman-Mintzer, O., & Ballenger, J. C. (1996). Recent developments in the psychopharmacology of anxiety disorders. *Journal of Consulting and Clinical Psychology, 64*(4), 660–668.

Malkoff-Schwartz, S., Frank, E., Anderson, B. P., Hlastala, S. A., Luther, J. F., Sherrill, J. T., Houck, P. R., & Kupfer, D. J. (2000). Social rhythm disruption and stressful life events in the onset of bipolar and unipolar episodes. *Psychological Medicine, 30,* 1005–1016.

Martinsen, E. W., Hoffart, A., & Solberg, O. (1989). Comparing aerobic with nonaerobic forms of exercise in the treatment of clinical depression: a randomized trial. *Comprehensive Psychiatry, 30*(4), 324–331.

McNally, R. (2002). Anxiety sensitivity and panic disorder. *Biological Psychiatry, 52,* 938–946.

McNeil, J. K., LeBlanc, E. M., & Joyner, M. (1991). The effect of exercise on depressive symptoms in the moderately depressed elderly. *Psychology & Aging, 6,* 487–488.

Merikangas, K. R., Akiskal, H. S., Angst, J., Greenberg, P. E., Hirschfeld, R. M. A., Petukhova, M., et al. (2007). Lifetime and 12-month prevalence of bipolar spectrum disorder in the national comorbidity survey replication. *Archives of General Psychiatry, 64*(5), 543–552.

Ng, F., Dodd, S., & Berk, M. (2007). The effects of physical activity in the acute treatment of bipolar disorder: A pilot study. *Journal of Affective Disorders, 101,* 259–262.

Otto, M. W., & Miklowitz, D. J. (2004). The role and impact of psychotherapy in the management of bipolar disorder. *CNS Spectrums, 9*(11 Suppl 12), 27–32.

Otto, M. W., Pollack, M. H., Fava, M., & Uccello, R. (1995). Elevated anxiety sensitivity index scores in patients with major depression: Correlates and changes with antidepressant treatment. *Journal of Anxiety Disorders, 9*(2), 117–123.

Otto, M. W., Smits, J. A. J., & Reese, H. E. (2005). Combined psychotherapy and pharmacotherapy for mood and anxiety disorders in adults: Review and analysis. *Clinical Psychology: Science and Practice, 12*(1), 72–86.

Paffenbarger, R. S., Jr., Lee, I. M., & Leung, R. (1994). Physical activity and personal characteristics associated with depression and suicide in American college men. *Acta Psychiatrica Scandanavia, 89* (Suppl 377), 16–22.

Pagliari, R., & Peyrin, L. (1995). Norepinephrine release in the rat frontal cortex under treadmill exercise: A study with microdialysis. *Journal of Applied Physiology, 78*, 2121–2130.

Petruzzello, S. J., Landers, D. M., Hatfield, B. D., Kubitz, K. A., & Salazar, W. (1991). A meta-analysis on the anxiety-reducing effects of acute and chronic exercise. Outcomes and mechanisms. *Sports Medicine, 11*(3), 143–182.

Pinchasov, B. B., Shurgaja, A. M., Grischin, O. V., & Putilov, A. A. (2000). Mood and energy regulation in seasonal and non-seasonal depression before and after midday treatment with physical exercise or bright light. *Psychiatry Research, 94 (1)*, 29–42.

Reiss, S., Peterson, R. P., Gursky, D. M., & McNally, R. J. (1986). Anxiety sensitivity, anxiety frequency, and the prediction of fearfulness. *Behavior Research and Therapy, 24*, 1–8.

Ronald C. Kessler, PhD; Patricia Berglund, MBA; Olga Demler, MA, MS; Robert Jin, MA; Kathleen R. Merikangas, PhD; Ellen E. Walters, MS.

Ronald C. Kessler, PhD; Wai Tat Chiu, AM; Olga Demler, MA, MS; Ellen E. Walters, MS.

Roy-Byrne, P. P., Davidson, K. W., Kessler, R. C., Asmundson, G. J. G., Goodwin, R. D., Kubzansky, L., et al. (2008). Anxiety disorders and comorbid medical illness. *General Hospital Psychiatry, 30*(3), 208–225.

Rush, A. J., Bernstein, I. H., Trivedi M. H., Carmody, T. J., Wisniewski S., Mundt, J. C., et al. (2006). An evaluation of the quick inventory of depressive symptomatology and the Hamilton rating scale for depression: A sequenced treatment alternatives to relieve depression trial report. *Biological Psychiatry, 59*, 493–501.

Salmon, P. (2001). Effects of physical exercise on anxiety, depression, and sensitivity to stress: A unifying theory. *Clinical Psychology Review, 21*, 33–61.

Schmitz, N., Kruse, J., & Kugler, J. (2004). The association between physical exercises and health-related quality of life in subjects with mental disorders. Results from a cross-sectional survey. *Preventive Medicine, 39*(6), 1200–1207.

Schmidt, N. B., Lerew, D. R., Santiago, H., Trakowski, J. H, & Staab, J. P. (2000). Effects of heart-rate feedback on estimated cardiovascular fitness in patients with panic disorder. *Depression and Anxiety, 12*, 59–66.

Schmidt, N. B., Zvolensky, M. Z., & Maner, J. K. (2006). Anxiety sensitivity: Prospective prediction of panic attacks and Axis I pathology. *Journal of Psychiatric Research, 40*, 691–699.

Sexton, H., Maere, A., & Dahl, N. H. (1989). Exercise intensity and reduction of neurotic symptoms: a controlled follow-up study. *Acta Psychiatrica Scandinavica, 80(3)*, 231–235.

Simon, G. E. (2003). Social and economic burden of mood disorders. *Biological Psychiatry, 54*(3), 208–215.

Simon, N. M., Otto, M. W., Fischmann, D., Racette, S., Nierenberg, A. A., Pollack, M. H, et al., (2005). Panic disorder and bipolar disorder: Anxiety sensitivity as a potential mediator of panic during manic states. *Journal of Affective Disorders, 87*(1), 101–105.

Singh, N. A., Clements, K. M., & Fiatarone, M. A. (1997). A randomized controlled trial of the effect of exercise on sleep. *Sleep, 20*(2), 95–101.

Singh, N. A., Stavrinos, T. M., Scarbek, Y., Galambos, G., Liber, C. L., & Fiatarone Singh, M. (2005). A randomized controlled trial of high versus low intensity weight training versus general practitioner care for clinical depression in older adults. *Journal of Gerontology: Medical Sciences, 60A*, 768–776.

Smits, J. A., Berry, A. C., Rosenfield, D., Powers, M. B., Behar, E., & Otto, M. W. (2008). Reducing anxiety sensitivity with exercise. *Depress Anxiety, 25*(8), 689–699.

Smits, J. A. J., & Zvolensky, M. J. (2006). Emotional vulnerability as a function of physical activity among individuals with panic disorder. *Depress Anxiety, 23*, 102–106.

Stathopoulou, G., Powers, M. B., Berry, A. C., Smits, J. A. J, & Otto M.W. (2006). Exercise interventions for mental health: A quantitative and qualitative review. *Clinical Psychology: Science and Practice, 13*, 179–193.

Stephens, T. (1988). Physical activity and mental health in the United States and Canada: Evidence from four population surveys. *Preventive Medicine, 17*(1), 35–47.

Stewart, W. F., Ricci, J. A., Chee, E., Hahn, S. R., & Morganstein, D. (2003). Cost of lost productive work time among US workers with depression. *JAMA: Journal of the American Medical Association, 289*(23), 3135–3144.

Tanaka, H., & Shirakawa, S. (2004). Sleep health, lifestyle and mental health in the Japanese elderly: Ensuring sleep to promote a healthy brain and mind. *Journal of Psychosomatic Research, 56*(5), 465–477.

Tang, T. Z., & DeRubeis, R. J. (1999). Sudden gains and critical sessions in cognitive-behavioral therapy for depression. *Journal of Consulting and Clinical Psychology, 67*(6), 894–904.

Tang, T. Z., DeRubeis, R. J., Hollon, S. D., Amsterdam, J., & Shelton, R. (2007). Sudden gains in cognitive therapy of depression and depression relapse/recurrence. *Journal of Consulting and Clinical Psychology, 75*(3), 404–408.

Taylor, S., Koch, W. J., & McNally, R. J. (1992). How does anxiety sensitivity vary across the anxiety disorders? *Journal of Anxiety Disorders, 6,* 249–259.

Teasdale, J. D. (1983). Negative thinking in depression: Cause, effect or reciprocal relationship? *Advances in Behaviour Research and Therapy, 5,* 3–25.

Teasdale, J. D. (1988). Cognitive vulnerability to persistent depression. *Cognition and Emotion, 2,* 247–274.

Thase, M. E., & Denko, T. (2008). Pharmacotherapy of mood disorders. *Annual Review of Clinical Psychology, 4,* 53–91.

Veale, D., Le Fevre, K., Pantelis, C., De Souza, V., Mann, A., & Sargeant, A. (1992). Aerobic exercise in the adjunctive treatment of depression: a randomized controlled trial. *Journal of the Royal Society Medicine, 85,* 541–544.

Vogel, G. W. (1983). Evidence for REM sleep deprivation as the mechanism of action of antidepressant drugs. *Progress in Neuropsychopharmacology & Biological Psychiatry, 7,* 343–349.

Zaretsky, A., Segal, Z., & Gemar, M. (1999). Cognitive therapy for bipolar depression: A pilot study. *Canadian Journal of Psychiatry, 44,* 491–494.

About the Authors

Jasper A. J. Smits, PhD, is Assistant Professor of Psychology and Director of the Anxiety Research and Treatment Program at Southern Methodist University in Dallas. He is an expert in the treatment of anxiety and mood disorders, and he has been at the forefront of research investigating both the mechanism and the dissemination of successful cognitive-behavioral treatment strategies. He has also specialized in the link between anxiety, illness, and health behaviors (e.g., exercise and smoking) and in the evaluation of novel treatment strategies for anxiety patients. His research is funded by the National Institute of Mental Health and he has published over 50 scientific works, including a recent coedited book *Anxiety in Health Behaviors and Physical Illness*. His current exercise routine includes regular running, tennis, and biking. He recently completed his first triathlon and is planning more.

Michael W. Otto, PhD, is Professor of Psychology and Director of the Center for Anxiety and Related Disorders at Boston University. He specializes in the treatment of mood, anxiety, and substance use disorders. Dr. Otto's research focuses on difficult-to-treat populations, including the application of cognitive-behavioral strategies to patients who have failed to respond to previous interventions, as well as on developing novel treatment strategies for bipolar disorder and substance use disorders. He has published over 250 scientific articles, chapters, and books spanning his research interests and was recently identified as a "top producer" in the clinical empirical literature. Dr. Otto is past President of the Association for Behavioral and Cognitive Therapies (formerly AABT), a fellow of the American Psychological Association, and a member of the Scientific Advisory Board for the Anxiety Disorders Association of America. For exercise, he currently devotes effort to indoor rock climbing, outdoor running, and occasional time in the swimming pool.